T0086143

POCKET **ROUGH GUIDE**

JERSEY

WEEKENDER

YOUR TAILOR-MADE TRIP
STARTS HERE

Tailor-made trips and unique adventures crafted by local experts

Rough Guides has been inspiring travellers with lively and thought-provoking guidebooks for more than 35 years. Now we're linking you up with selected local experts to craft your dream trip. They will put together your perfect itinerary and book it at local rates.

Don't follow the crowd – find your own path.

HOW ROUGHGUIDES.COM/TRIPS WORKS

STEP 1

Pick your dream destination, tell us what you want and submit an enquiry.

STEP 2

Fill in a short form to tell your local expert about your dream trip and preferences.

STEP 3

Our local expert will craft your tailor-made itinerary. You'll be able to tweak and refine it until you're completely satisfied.

STEP 4

Book online with ease, pack your bags and enjoy the trip! Our local expert will be on hand 24/7 while you're on the road.

BENEFITS OF PLANNING AND BOOKING AT ROUGHGUIDES.COM/TRIPS

PLAN YOUR ADVENTURE WITH LOCAL EXPERTS

Rough Guides' English-speaking local experts are hand-picked, based on their experience in the travel industry and their impeccable standards of customer service.

SAVE TIME AND GET ACCESS TO LOCAL KNOWLEDGE

When a local expert plans your trip, you save time and money when you book, even during high season. You won't be charged for using a credit card either.

MAKE TRAVEL A BREEZE: BOOK WITH PEACE OF MIND

Enjoy stress-free travel when you use Rough Guides' secure online booking platform. All bookings come with a money-back guarantee.

WHAT DO OTHER TRAVELLERS THINK ABOUT ROUGH GUIDES TRIPS?

Trip to Spain

This Spain tour company did a fantastic job to make our dream trip perfect. We gave them our travel budget, told them where we would like to go, and they did all of the planning. Our drivers and tour guides were always on time and very knowledgable. The hotel accommodations were better than we would have found on our own. Only one time did we end up in a location that we had not intended to be in. We called the 24 hour phone number, and they immediately fixed the situation.

Don A, USA ★★★★★

Trip to Morocco

Our trip was fantastic! Transportation, accommodations, guides – all were well chosen! The hotels were well situated, well appointed and had helpful, friendly staff. All of the guides we had were very knowledgeable, patient, and flexible with our varied interests in the different sites. We particularly enjoyed the side trip to Tangier! Well done! The itinerary you arranged for us allowed maximum coverage of the country with time in each city for seeing the important places.

Sharon, USA ★★★★★

PLAN AND BOOK YOUR TRIP AT ROUGHGUIDES.COM/TRIPS

CONTENTS

10 Things not to miss

Spectacular cliff paths, stunning coastal scenery, beautiful gardens, historic forts and castles, and museums chronicling the island's rich heritage – here are just some of the highlights of Jersey at a glance.

∧ **Jersey War Tunnels.** The dark, dank tunnels and evocative displays are a harrowing reminder of Jersey under the Germans. See page 32

∧ **Elizabeth Castle.** Take the Castle Ferry to see this Tudor fort, which defended the island for over 300 years. See page 25

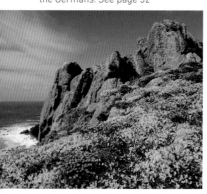

∧ **North Coast Footpath.** Flower-clad cliff paths extend all along the northern coast, offering bracing walks and stunning views. See page 79

> **Maritime Museum.** Explore the island's links with the sea and its former role as a seafaring state. See page 17

∧ **Mont Orgueil Castle.** Climb the ramparts of this medieval fortress for splendid views of the east coast and Normandy, across the water. See page 89

∧ **Samarès Manor.** This fine manor is a horticultural haven with acres of landscaped gardens, a plant nursery and spectacular herb garden. See page 96

∧ **Jersey Museum and Art Gallery.** Steep yourself in Jersey's history at this award-winning museum. See page 24

∨ **Surfing.** Ride the big Atlantic swell which pounds the 4-mile (6km) sandy bay of St Ouen's – or just sit and watch the surfing pros. See page 49

∨ **La Hougue Bie.** A huge mound conceals one of the largest and best-preserved Neolithic passage graves in Europe. See page 88

∨ **Jersey Zoo.** No ordinary zoo, Durrell has been saving species on the brink for more than 60 years. See page 100

INTRODUCTION TO
Jersey
A tiny island in the shadow of France, Jersey packs in big beaches, stunning seascapes and a host of historic and family attractions.

When the novelist Victor Hugo was exiled from France he chose to live on the island closest to home – just 14 miles (22km) across the Channel, where his native language was spoken. "Fragments of Europe dropped by France and picked up by England",

was how he described the Channel Islands. As self-governing islands and strongholds of ancient, semi-feudal laws, the Channel Islands are neither truly British, nor are they French. English is now the accepted language, the currency is pounds and pence, yet many street names are still in French, the food has a Gallic slant and the islands have a distinctly foreign flavour. Tourists are drawn by this combination of French flavour and British lifestyle – not to mention the location, which is sufficiently far south to guarantee more daily hours of sun than anywhere else in Britain.

For a small island, Jersey offers a wide range of attractions and activities, from ancient castles and wartime relics to sea sports and cycle tours, spas and adventure parks. But for most visitors it's the coastline that has the greatest allure. Jersey has 50 miles (80km) of shoreline and 20 miles (32km) of fine sandy beaches, swept clean by huge tides. The island tilts southwards, and seascapes range from the towering cliffs of the north to the Atlantic rollers of the west and the spacious sands of the south. The island has one of the largest tidal movements in the world, and the coastal landscape undergoes dramatic changes between high and low water.

Location and Climate

The most southerly of the British Isles, Jersey lies in the Gulf of St Malo, 100 miles (160km) from mainland Britain, but only 14 miles (22km) from the coast of Normandy. On most days you can see France from the north and east coasts. Largest of the Channel Islands, Jersey is 9 miles (14km) east to west, 5 miles (8km) north to south. In summer, the island has a daily average of eight hours of sunshine and an enviable average maximum temperature of 68°F (20°C). There

is always the risk of bad weather, but clouds are often quickly dispersed by the strong south-westerly winds.

The Jersey cow pops up everywhere on the island.

Toads and Donkeys

Deep-rooted rivalries exist between Jersey and Guernsey. To Guernsey natives Jersey is "the other island" and the inhabitants are *crapauds* (toads), while Jersey people refer to the residents of their supposedly stubborn little sister as *ânes* (donkeys).

The *crapaud*, which is found only on Jersey, has been fast disappearing from ponds and waterways. The Durrell Wildlife Conservation Trust, renowned for recovering endangered species from more exotic climes, is currently helping to save the island mascot.

British Links

The Channel Islands once formed part of the Duchy of Normandy but have had links with the British Isles ever since the Battle of Hastings, when they became part of the Anglo-Norman realm. The links were reinforced in 1204 when King John lost Normandy to France but the Channel Islands chose to remain loyal to the English crown. In return for their allegiance King John granted the islands customs and privileges, tantamount to self-government, which have since been confirmed by every English monarch. France then became the enemy, and for the next 650 years Jersey was repeatedly threatened by French invasions. The last invaders were the Nazi Germans, who occupied the Channel Islands in World War II.

Language

Until the 1960s French was still the official language of Jersey. Prayers are still said in French before States and court sittings, and the parliament votes *pour* or *contre*. Not so long ago a Jersey resident would have spoken English, standard French and Jèrriais, a derivation of ancient Jersey-Norman. This *patois* enjoyed a revival during the German Occupation as a useful means of covert communication, and today it can very occasionally be heard by elderly Jersiais (the people who speak it). Only a handful of the population speak it fluently, but renewed interest in the language has led to the introduction of classes in some schools.

The English language was first introduced to Jersey in the eighteenth century, and is now spoken by all the islanders. Street names on the island still carry their French names, often very different from the English names

Jersey Royals are one of the most prized crops of spring.

Anne Port, a pleasant cove on the northeast of the island, is an ideal location for rockpooling with children.

they were later given, eg La Rue de Derrière (King Street) or La Rue des Trois Pigeons (Hill Street).

Economy

The all-dominant financial services industry accounts for over 40 percent of the total economic activity on Jersey, employing around a fifth of the workforce. This took over from agriculture and tourism as the mainstay of the economy in the latter part of the twentieth century. Tourism generates less than 4 percent of Jersey's GVA though the total impact of the sector is equivalent to 8.3 percent of GVA, and it accounts for over 8% of the island's employment. The decade-long downward trend in travel to Jersey was reversed in 2017 when the island saw 727,000 visits, putting it on track to achieve its aim of one million visitors by 2030.

Since Napoleonic times Jersey has attracted high-earning immigrants seeking to benefit from the island's desirable way of life and advantageous tax laws. Today's high earners are actively encouraged through the High Value Residency initiative, whereby applications are assessed for suitability on social and economic grounds, including paying a minimum tax of £145,000 per annum.

Environment

Jersey has a growing number of over twenty Sites of Special Interest (SSIs), 28 of them protected for ecological and 22 for their geological interest, plus a huge intertidal zone designated as a Ramsar site (a wetland of international importance) on the southeast coast. The island's sixteen beaches are washed by some of the cleanest waters in Europe.

Green lanes, reducing the speed limit on some country lanes to 15mph (24kmh), have encouraged cyclists and pedestrians, and clearly marked cycle routes now cover around 100 miles (161km) of coast and countryside. On the negative side, although the island is still largely unspoilt, its capital St Helier has seen very unsightly development swallowing the coastline. The amount of rubbish generated has doubled in two decades and the island only recycles a third of its waste. Jersey still has one of the highest car ownership and user rates in the world. It's remarkable how many Porsches and other fast cars you see given that the maximum speed limit on the island is 40mph (64kmh)!

Food and Drink

Jersey has a thriving gastronomic scene and the islanders are spoilt for choice. Within its 45-mile (70km) radius there are around two hundred restaurants, including several listed in the Michelin Guide. A vast array of fabulously fresh seafood and fish is caught around the shores, and that's not the only local produce. Jersey produces its own vegetables, fruit, herbs, beef, pork and even cheeses. Not to mention the famous Jersey Royal potatoes and the rich creamy milk from Jersey cows.

For the islanders fishing has always been a way of life. In the Middle Ages the abundance of conger eel, which was salted, dried and shipped to England, led to the nickname "Isle of the Congers". From the sixteenth century fortunes were made from the cod banks of Newfoundland. Conger numbers have declined, but lobsters, scallops, crabs, bass, mackerel and grey mullet are still fished from Jersey shores, and around 4 million oysters are farmed annually at the Royal Bay of Grouville.

A hearty bowl of traditional Jersey bean crock.

The island works hard to promote its food with an annual food festival and the two-month Tennerfest in October-November when over one hundred restaurants offer fixed-price menus. Prosperous resident financiers and lawyers keep the upmarket restaurants in business, and even the discerning French come across the Channel to indulge their palates. St Helier boasts the Michelin-starred Bohemia (see

The Jersey Ormer

The indigenous ormer, related to the abalone, is now so rare that fishing is only permitted between October and April on the first day of each new or full moon, and the five days following. Ormers cooked in a casserole with belly of pork, shallots and carrot used to be a daily dish, the mother-of-pearl shell used as an ashtray or thrown away. Occasionally you'll see locals scouring the rocks for the prized molluscs, but long gone are the days when they featured on restaurant menus.

The iridescent ear-shaped shell of the ormer.

page 31) and excellent Samphire, among others, at Beaumont there's the Bib Gourmand-awarded Mark Jordan at the Beach; St Aubin, St Brelade and Gorey all have excellent choices, from smart seafood restaurants to beachside cafés serving home-made cakes and Jersey cream teas. Even in tiny Rozel, right up in the north, you can choose between a legendary crab sandwich at the Hungry Man kiosk or hand-dived scallops at The Rozel. Meanwhile, at Green Island Beach in the southeast you'll find the Mediterranean-influenced Green Island, which makes the most of the island's seafood and seasonal ingredients and might just lay claim to being the southernmost restaurant in the British Isles.

Island Specialities

A few island favourites survive from bygone days. The misleadingly named **black butter** *(du nièr beurre)* is an apple preserve that used to be made in vast quantities every autumn. Typical recipes comprised 700lb of apples, 10 gallons of cider, 20lb of sugar, 24 lemons and 3lb of spices. Cooking carried on all day and night, with family members stirring the huge pot and making merry with song and dance. La Mare Vineyards (see page 62) make their own black butter and sell it at their estate and at St Helier market.

Just occasionally you come across **Jersey bean crock**, a variation of the French cassoulet, comprising five different kinds of dried beans, pig's trotter, belly of pork or shin of beef, carrot and onion. The hearty dish is served with cabbage loaf, a crusty white bread baked in large cabbage leaves. At festivals and other island events look out for *les mèrvelles* or Jersey Wonders, doughnut-like cakes in the shape of an 8 – traditionally cooked as the tide goes out.

Jersey Fizz

Cider used to be the island tipple, and large quantities were exported from the mid-seventeenth century to the mid-nineteenth century. One of the few places where cider is made today is La Mare Wine Estate, which produces a sparkling form, similar to the Normandy *cidre bouché*. La Mare is on the same latitude as Champagne and produces the very palatable sparkling white Le Mourier, using the *méthode traditionelle*.

Eating Out Price Guide

Prices are based on a two-course meal for one person, including a glass of wine.

£ = under £25
££ = £25–40
£££ = over £40

Jersey cows provide many tasty local treats.

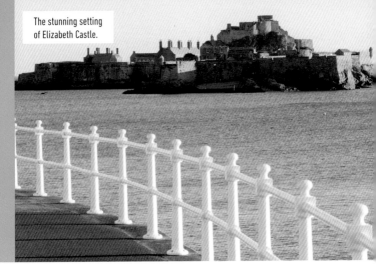

The stunning setting of Elizabeth Castle.

TOUR 1

St Helier

This walk around Jersey's capital, visiting two of the best museums, the lively Central Market and historic Elizabeth Castle, is 2½ miles (4km) and takes a whole day.

Jersey's capital is home to two of the best museums on the island, a spectacularly located historic castle and a central square steeped in history. Although the traffic in the capital is worse than anywhere else on the island, the main shopping thoroughfares, with large stores, boutiques and lively food markets, are pedestrianised. The walk takes you through the historic centre, west to Elizabeth Castle and back along the waterfront.

The town's origins date back to the sixth century when Helerius, a monk from modern-day Belgium, founded a hermitage on a small rocky outcrop on a tidal islet in St Aubin's Bay, today known as the Hermitage Rock. Helerius devoted his life to prayer and

Highlights

- Maritime Museum and Occupation Tapestry Gallery
- Royal Square
- Central Market and Fish Market
- Jersey Museum and Art Gallery
- Elizabeth Castle

fasting, but in AD 555, after fifteen years on the island, he was beheaded by a band of passing pirates. A small monastic settlement rose up here, and in the twelfth century, an oratory was dedicated to St Helier.

Growth over the centuries was slow and it was not until entrepreneurial Huguenot refugees arrived in the sixteenth and seventeenth centuries,

Hermitage Rock.

had taken over from St Aubin as the island's main harbour.

Liberation Square

Start at **Liberation Square** ❶, which was opened by Prince Charles on 9 May 1995, the fiftieth anniversary of the Liberation of the island from German Occupation. It was here that jubilant crowds greeted the British liberators after five long years under German rule. To mark the seventieth anniversary of Liberation in May 2015, Jersey and the other Channel Islands celebrated with a host of entertainment and activities, stretching over five weeks.

The prominent **Liberation Sculpture** commemorates the event with a bronze group of figures, holding up the Union flag. From left to right the figures represent a Jersey couple old enough to have witnessed the Occupation, a liberator, a Jersey fisherman and a farmer with his wife and children. Overlooking the square on the north side, the Pomme d'Or Hotel was the headquarters of the German navy during the Occupation.

The square used to be the terminus of the Jersey Railway which served the south and east coasts, and

bringing their skills with them, that the town saw any real expansion. Further growth came about in the late 18th century, funded by all the profits from privateering during the French and American wars. In the post-Napoleonic era, the population was swelled when hundreds of officers from the English army settled in the town. Retired on half pay, they were lured to Jersey by the climate, the low cost of living and the desirable lifestyle. Regency and Victorian houses were constructed, land was reclaimed from the sea, and by 1840 St Helier

The bronze Liberation Sculpture in Liberation Square.

The Maritime Museum on New North Quay.

it was from the rear of the building on the west side that some 2,200 residents were deported to Germany in September 1942.

Alongside Liberation Square is Liberty Wharf, a covered shopping mall of independent boutiques and major brand stores within original granite warehouses.

Maritime Museum and Tapestry Gallery

Across the busy A1 south of Liberation Square, and looking like something

16 New Street

Originally the home of a public notary, the early Georgian House at 16 New Street has served as the HQ of the Liberty Gentlemen's Club and latterly the workshop of de Gruchy, the Jersey department store. By the 1980s it was neglected and demolition was threatened. However, the National Trust bought the property for £1 in 2003 and thanks to a £1 million bequest by the late Mollie Houston, who moved to Jersey after WWII, the Trust was able to undertake a meticulous renovation.

out of Disneyland, the world's largest **Steam Clock** is modelled on a nineteenth-century paddle steamer. Local vessels and shipbuilders are commemorated on benches around the harbour. The facade of the otherwise drab Normans building across the old harbour is the canvas for Jersey's most ambitious piece of street art, 'Home', a collaboration between ArtHouse Jersey and Walthamstow-based Wood Street Walls. Designed by British street artist Gabriel Pitcher, this huge mural celebrates the contribution of immigrant communities to the island, and is just one of the many striking pieces of street art dotted around the city, forming part of the St Helier Art Trail (https://www.jersey.com/inspire-me/inspiration/st-helier-art-trail).

The nearby **Maritime Museum** ❷, (www.jerseyheritage.org; Mar–Nov), housed in a restored warehouse on **New North Quay**, explores every aspect of the island's links with the sea. Jersey was one of the largest shipbuilding centres in Europe, its shipyards around the coast producing over eight hundred wooden sailing ships in the mid-nineteenth century. From the 1860s the trade suffered from the advent of iron and steam.

This first-rate museum offers a host of hands-on exhibits and other

Salty sea dogs in the Maritime Museum.

There are 12 richly embroidered tapestries in the Occupation Tapestry Gallery, detailing the moving story of life in Jersey during World War II.

activities for visitors of all ages. You can feel the pull of the currents and the power of the sea, design a boat and listen to songs and salty tales of the past. Among the highlights are a full-size replica of the bow of the Jersey-built brig, the *Orient Star*, and the 'Voyages Globe', a giant animatronic globe illustrating the journeys of Jersey's ships all over the world. On Mondays, Tuesdays and Wednesdays you can watch the declining art of boat-building as volunteers repair and maintain the museum's fleet of historic vessels. Examples of the restored boats can sometimes be seen in the marina outside the museum.

Occupation Tapestry Gallery

Within the museum is the **Occupation Tapestry Gallery ❸** comprising twelve separate large tapestries charting the story of the Occupation from the arrival of the Germans to their surrender to the British liberators in 1945.

These historically accurate and meticulously worked scenes were created by the twelve Jersey parishes to commemorate the 50th anniversary of Liberation. Themes range from 'The Outbreak of War' and 'Deportation'

to 'The Daily Life of Civilians', such as the school-room scene of a boy yawning in a German lesson.

Return to Liberation Square, cross the Esplanade on the far side and take Mulcaster Street. About halfway up the road you'll see the **Lamplighter Pub**, decorated with stuccowork depicting the figure of Britannia between two cherubs and a garland of fruit below. This was the work of Turnkey Giffard, a prison warden who entertained his inmates by showing them how to carve. Take

Looking up to the square tower of the Church of St Helier.

the next turning left into **Bond Street**, where Regency and Victorian buildings retain some of their original features.

Church of St Helier

On the right stands the pink granite **Church of St Helier** ❹ (normally open during daylight hours), the largest of the parish churches. The seafront used to come right up to the church, and the square tower served as a useful observation post. The stretch of land between here and the sea was reclaimed from the end of the eighteenth century for town housing and warehouses.

> ## St Helier
>
> The hermit Helerius was murdered by axe-wielding Saxon pirates. He was later canonised, and his death is commemorated by the pair of crossed axes which feature on the St Helier parish crest. According to local folklore, after Helerius was murdered, he picked up his severed head and carried it for 200 metres/yds to the shore. Every year on the Sunday closest to 16 July, St Helier's day, a procession makes its way to the Hermitage Rock and a wreath is laid at the entrance of the oratory which was built over his cave.

The gate at the far end of the railings formed part of a screen used to segregate male and female prisoners during services in the Debtors' Prison. Major Peirson, hero of the Battle of Jersey (see page 21), is buried in the centre of the church, while Baron de Rullecourt, who led the enemy, merely has a simple memorial in the churchyard; the location of his grave is unknown.

Streets and sewers

Leave the church by the north side for **Church Street**. The name of the street looks somewhat prosaic beside the former French name, **La Rue Trousse Cotillon** or Pick Up Your Petticoat Street. The name dates from a less salubrious era when ladies had to lift up their dresses to avoid the drains and sewers. English settlers in St Helier in the mid-nineteenth century replaced some of the French street names with English alternatives that had no connection at all with the originals.

It was in the house on the opposite side of the road (now the United Club) where John Wesley, founder of Methodism, preached the Gospel in 1787. Wesley, who visited Jersey, Guernsey and Alderney, had a

Annual pilgrimage to Hermitage Rock.

Bullet holes, fired by troops in the 1781 Battle of Jersey, can still be seen in the walls of the Peirson Pub in the now peaceful Royal Square.

profound influence on the islanders, and by the 1820s chapels, large and small, in the vernacular Gothic or classical styles, were appearing all over the islands. The **St Helier Methodist Centre** (formerly the Wesley Grove Methodist Church) at the top of Halkett Place used to seat 1,600. Methodism still has a strong influence on many of the islanders and several of the churches are still in use.

Further along on the corner is **Jersey's first library**, a Georgian building and one of the first on the island to be made of brick. At the end of Library Place, to the left, the **obelisk** was erected in 1855 to Pierre le Sueur, the Constable of St Helier who transformed the town by ridding the streets of streams of sewage, providing clean water, and installing a complete underground system.

Royal Square

Retrace your steps to Church Street, turning left into **Royal Square ❺**, formerly the Market Place, where weekly markets-cum-fairs took place, prisoners awaited trial in a cage (public executions took place nearby) and where, on occasions, witches were burnt. Devil worship had spread to Jersey by the late sixteenth century, and

witch trials were common. The sentence for a convicted witch was 'to be hanged and strangled by the public executioner till death ensues, after that her body to be burned and entirely consumed'.

The name Market Place was changed to Royal Square in honour of King George II (1727–60), who donated £200 towards the creation of St Helier's first harbour. An ostentatious statue of the king in the square shows him dressed as Caesar. Below the statue a proclamation stone commemorates the day in February 1649 when Jersey proclaimed Charles

The gilded statue of George II, posing as Caesar, in Royal Square.

Attractive 17th-century houses are now home to jewellers' shops.

II King of England, after the execution of his father. During the English Civil War, the island had provided Charles with refuge on two occasions, the first time as the young Prince of Wales. He was not crowned king in England until 1660, and for over ten years he was acknowledged as the rightful king only in Jersey and Scotland. As a reward for Jersey's loyalty, Charles gave Smith's Island and some neighbouring islets off Virginia to Sir George Carteret with permission to settle. Carteret renamed them New Jersey.

Battle of Jersey

In the centre of Royal Square a stone commemorates the Battle of Jersey, which took place in 1781. A French force of 600, led by Baron de Rullecourt, secretly landed at night on the southeastern tip of the island, at La Rocque. The Lieutenant-Governor of Jersey, Moses Corbet, who was still in bed, surrendered, tricked into believing that the French had an overwhelming army. But the British soldiers and Jersey Militia refused to lay down their arms and a heroic young English officer, Major Francis Peirson, led the local troops to victory in a brief but bloody battle in Royal Square. Both de Rullecourt and Peirson were killed

in action. This was the last attempt by France to capture the island. The young hero was immortalised in John Singleton Copley's painting of *The Death of Major Peirson* at London Tate Britain Gallery, a copy of which hangs in the Royal Court on Royal Square.

Royal Square today

Today Royal Square is a peaceful, shady spot, providing a retreat from the town traffic and alfresco pubs and cafés where. you can sit with a drink and watch the world go by. The building nearest to Church Street is the former **Corn Market**, preserving the original granite arches inside and now home to the Registry Office.

If you look carefully at the paving stones on this side of the square you'll see a carved 'V' for Victory. This was cut by a local stonemason while relaying the stones during the German Occupation. Discovery could have led to deportation, so he hid the 'V' under a layer of sand. The letters 'EGA' and '1945' were added after the Swedish Red Cross ship, the SS *Vega*, arrived towards the end of the Occupation with 750 tons of food parcels, relieving the islanders from near-starvation.

Jersey's Constitution

The constitution of the States of Jersey comprises the offices of Bailiff, Lieutenant-Governor, who is the monarch's representative on the island, the Dean of Jersey, the Attorney General and the Solicitor General – along with 8 senators, 12 parish constables and 29 deputies who are all democratically elected. The old committee system was abolished in 2005 and ministerial government introduced. A number of scrutiny panels keep an eye on the policies of the executive.

The Royal Court

On the south side of Royal Square, the central building is the **Royal Court** (1866), the island's court of justice, with the arms of George II above the entrance. It was from the balcony to the right that Alexander Coutanche, Bailiff of Jersey, hoisted the Union flag on 8 May 1945 and relayed to the huge crowds Churchill's message that the Channel Islands were to be liberated. East of here is the **States Chamber**, the island's parliament.

Central Market

Peirson Place, beside the pub, leads to King Street (formerly Rue Derrière), a busy pedestrianised shopping thoroughfare. Turn right along King Street for Halkett Place, named after a former Lieutenant-Governor of Jersey who served with distinction at the Battle of Waterloo. Cross the street and turn left for the **Central Market** ❻ (Mon–Sat). Market stalls were banned from Royal Square in 1800 and a new site chosen on the corner of Halkett Place and Beresford Street.

The original was a splendid grand building, modelled on the City of Bath market. But to celebrate the centenary of the Battle of Jersey a new market was constructed in 1881 – which is the one you see today. This is a fine glass-roofed building with a wonderful array of fresh produce, including strawberries, asparagus, Jersey herbs and home-grown flowers. Apart from fruit and veg there are butchers and bakers, cafés, restaurants and delis selling island specialities.

Outside the post office in the Central Market, the red hexagonal pillar box (1851) designed by the novelist Anthony Trollope, was, according to Jersey, the very first in the British Isles. They were originally painted green, and it wasn't until 1874 that the post boxes were painted the familiar red.

Watch out for giant lobsters at the Fish Market.

The Central Market entrance.

Fish Market

Leave the Central Market at the Beresford Street exit and turn right. Across the road, the **Fish Market** ❼ (also known as Beresford Market) has a spectacular selection of seafood and fish, both local and imported. Head down here at 7.30am to see the arrival of the catch of the day or make it later and enjoy a seafood lunch and glass of wine at The Blue Ocean within the market. From the Jersey waters come sea bass, wrasse, grey mullet, shrimps, live lobsters, spider and chancre crabs, bream and mackerel. Look out too for conger eels, though long gone are the days when these were caught in profusion around the Jersey shores. In the seventeenth century congers were so popular and abundant that the Channel Islands acquired the nickname of 'the Kingdom of Congers'.

Exit the Fish Market at its northern end, turn right along Minden Place and cross over Bath Street for the **Jersey Arts Centre** (www.artscentre.je), a short way along on the left. This provides a broad range of the performing and visual arts for all ages and has an excellent café serving food all day (see page 31). Return to Bath Street, turning left for the West Centre, where you'll meet a family of bronze Jersey cows, and a tiny toad or *crapaud*.

At the end of Bath Street, turn right into **Queen Street**, which with King Street, is the town's main shopping thoroughfare. The next left will bring you into Hill Street, the street of advocates bristling with brass nameplates. Turn right for Mulcaster Street and first left for Pier Road.

Just up the hill on the right is **La Société Jersiaise** (www.societe-jersiaise.org), founded in 1873 and dedicated to the study of the history, archaeology and natural history of the island, the conservation of the environment and historic buildings, and the establishment of an island museum.

Fresh market produce.

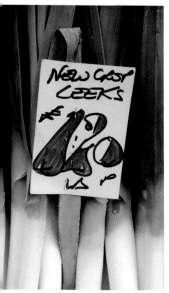

Jersey Museum and Art Gallery

Occupying a townhouse which used to stand on the seafront, the award-winning **Jersey Museum and Art Gallery** ❽ (www.jerseyheritage.org) gives you an excellent insight into Jersey life and history over the ages.

The house was built in 1818 by a wealthy shipowner who contributed in 1820 to the cost of land reclamation and a harbour-building scheme (now Commercial Buildings). The two upper floors have been lovingly restored and fitted out with period furniture to show how it would have looked like in Victorian times, when it was occupied by a doctor and his family.

The exhibition starts with a re-creation of the Old Stone Age site of La Cotte de St Brelade, showing the figures of Palaeolithic man on the rock face and the bones of prehistoric woolly rhino found at the foot of the cave. The finds at this Old Stone Age site prove that primitive man used the

Ancient remains on display at the Jersey Museum.

ravine as a 'funnel trap', charging the prehistoric beasts over the cliff edge to their deaths. On the same floor, don't miss the Story of Jersey film, with fascinating pre-war footage of Jersey; nor Lillie Langtry's immaculate Victorian travelling case.

Elizabeth Castle from Hermitage Rock.

The Jersey Lily

Highlights of Jersey Museum's art gallery are the two portraits of Lillie Langtry, by John Everett Millais and Sir Edward Poynter. Renowned for her beauty and pure white skin, she was nicknamed the Jersey Lily (the flower she is holding in Millais's painting is in fact a Guernsey not a Jersey lily). Both portraits caused a sensation at London's Royal Academy in 1878 – when Lillie was the acknowledged mistress of the Prince of Wales.

When Jersey's cave dwellers were stampeding rhino and mammoth off the clifftops Jersey was still attached to the Continent. A display on the first floor shows how the sea level rose and the Channel Islands were formed. A spectacular long torc in twisted gold, discovered in St Helier, hints at the prosperity of the Bronze Age, pre-2000 BC. Other exhibits cover the main events of the island's dramatic history as well as traditions and trades such as shipbuilding, knitting and oyster catching.

Elizabeth Castle

No visit to St Helier is really complete without a trip to **Elizabeth Castle ❾** one of Jersey's major historic monuments (www.jerseyheritage.org). Lying on an islet in St Aubin's Bay, the castle can be reached via the Esplanade, beyond Liberation Square, on the landward side. Follow signs for the tourist office, then continue on the Esplanade until you see the Castle Ferry kiosk on the waterfront. Visitors can either go by foot along the 0.6-mile (1km) causeway at low tide or catch the amphibious Castle Ferry (not included in the castle entrance fee), which travels at all tides.

Construction on the castle began in the late 16th century, by which time Mont Orgueil (see page 89), built for bows and arrows, was becoming increasingly exposed. Sir Walter Raleigh, the island's Governor, who lived at the castle from 1600, called it Fort Isabella Bellissima (Elizabeth the most Beautiful), in tribute to his Queen, Elizabeth I. It was not until the 1640s, when Jersey had been drawn into the English Civil War, that the castle – which by now had grown considerably in size – came into its own. Charles II, then Prince of Wales, took refuge here, and did so again after the execution of his father. During the war, Sir Philip Carteret, then Governor, resisted a siege here for 50 days, and the castle was the last

The Jersey Museum, a superb four-storey merchant's house.

Elizabeth Castle is accessible at all times by the amphibious Castle Ferry, or on foot at low tide.

of Jersey's strongholds to surrender. Defeat came in December 1651 when a shell from St Helier Hill (now Fort Regent) hit the abbey church and exploded the powder magazine. The Parliamentarians held Jersey for the next nine years.

Fit for a King

Follow in the footsteps of Sir Walter Raleigh and King Charles II and stay at Jersey's famous fortress. The small apartment (sleeping 4–6) within Elizabeth Castle may not be on the same scale as the Governor's house in the seventeenth century, but for those with a sense of adventure it's a wonderful spot to stay. Tides isolate the castle twice daily, but amphibious ferries provide a service during opening hours (bookings through Jersey Heritage at www.jerseyheritage.org).

Visiting the Castle

The fortifications you see today are divided into three: the oldest, **Upper Ward**, at the top, the **Lower Ward** beneath it and finally the **Outer Ward**. The oldest sections date from the 17th century, with the Guard House, hospital and workshops added in the early 19th century. The buildings around the **Parade Ground** house exhibitions covering the history of the castle, the development of the cannon and the story of the Royal Jersey Militia. The Militia served the island for around 600 years, and in their heyday numbered over six thousand local men, divided into five regiments. To reinforce the military theme, Gunner Graves fires the noonday gun.

From the Parade Ground it's easy to miss the access up to the older Upper Ward, also called the Mount. For the best views of the coast, climb up to the gunnery control tower. This was built by the Germans, who modernised the castle with bunkers and battlements.

Join in the re-enactment of the Gunner's Parade at Elizabeth Castle.

Over to the east you can see Fort Regent, which took over as the island's main fortress after Elizabeth Castle. Built into the mount is the Governor's

Aerial view of cottages on Les Minquiers.

house, where Sir Walter Raleigh lived – though he was off the island for most of his tenure.

On regular days throughout the season history is kept alive at the castle by displays of artillery, military parades and firing of the black powder cannons. There is plenty of audience participation, and visitors may be dragooned into drill practice and marching the Parade Ground!

Views to Fort Regent

Fort Regent, visible from Elizabeth Castle, was built in 1806–14 on a granite hill above St Helier and took over as the island's main fortress. It was built at enormous expense as a protection against further attacks from France. Napoleon had acted angrily over Jersey profiteering from French vessels: "France can tolerate no longer this nest of brigands and assassins. Europe must be purged of this vermin. Jersey is England's shame." Troops were stationed here

Les Minquiers

From Elizabeth Castle's gunnery control tower views stretch all the way south to Les Minquiers (known as 'The Minkies'), a group of rocky islets 9 miles (14km) offshore. Ownership of the reef and that of Les Ecréhous, the rocky islets between Jersey and Normandy, has on occasions been a matter of dispute between Jersey (backed by the UK) and France. In 1953 a battle was fought out at the International Court of Justice in The Hague. England won, much to the chagrin of the French. There are still occasional attempts to raise the Tricolore on the reefs, mainly by French fishermen asserting a claim to fishing rights off the islets.

General Conway's Dolmen

In 1785, during defence constructions on the hill where Fort Regent now stands, an extensive dolmen was discovered resembling a mini Stonehenge. Since the grave was impeding construction of the fort, it was presented as a retirement present to General Conway, then Governor of the island. The capstones and mighty megaliths – each weighing around 140 tons – were shipped across the Channel and taken up the Thames to grace the general's private estate upstream from Henley-on-Thames, where the dolmen stands today.

Plaque commemorating the dolmen, Vingtaine de la Ville.

for many years, but the French threat ended with the English victories at Trafalgar in 1805 and Waterloo in 1815, and the fort was never actually to fulfil its function. Today the most conspicuous feature of the fort is the modern white dome above the walls and bastions which survive from the original structure.

In 1958 the fort was sold back to the States of Jersey for £14,500, the original price of the land, and the building was then converted into a leisure centre.

La Frégate café, resembling an upturned boat, is part of St Helier's Waterfront.

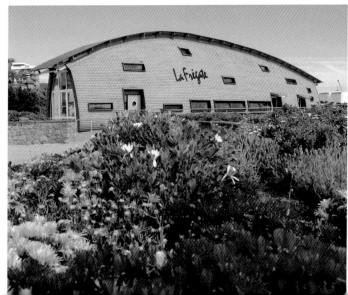

The signal station closed in 2005 through lack of funding, but a team from the Maritime Museum boat shop still maintains a signal system for strong gales – or flags to mark Liberation Day or Royal birthdays.

The Union flag on the west bastion is lowered to half-mast only when a monarch dies, though an exception was made on the death of Diana, Princess of Wales.

The Waterfront

As you leave Elizabeth Castle – whether by foot or amphibious craft – the views to the west are rather more alluring than those to the east.

Indeed, St Helier's **Waterfront** ❿ is Jersey's eyesore, characterised by a series of utilitarian high-rise buildings and large car parks. At drawing-board stage the aim was to 'breathe new life into the town and the island, enriching the quality of life for resident and visitor alike'. The leisure centre, clubs and fast-food outlets attract some of Jersey's younger residents, but others keep

Freedom Tree sculpture by Richard Perry, on the Waterfront.

The fort used to be the site of the last working signal station in the British Isles, used for weather warnings, high tides, shipping movements – and to indicate when the plane carrying national newspapers had left London and arrived in Jersey.

Musical entertainment draws a crowd at the Farm and Craft Market in St Helier.

Plain Sailing from St Helier

Cruising around the Jersey coast, racing a catamaran, spotting dolphins or seals, landing mackerel or sea bass or taking a ferry to France are all among the boating options. For visiting offshore reefs and seeing wildlife from a purpose-built rigid inflatable boat, go to www.jerseyseafaris.com. Standard cruise trips along 15 miles (24km) of the south coast depart from Albert Quay, St Helier.

Boats can be hired by the hour, day or week.

their distance, and there is little to attract the tourist.

The general feeling is that a huge potential has been sacrificed on the altar of the financial services sector, and that what could have been an attractive waterside, on the lines of other successful city waterfronts in Europe, is just there to provide housing, offices and parking for financiers.

To see for yourself, head south from the slipway, passing the upturned-boat

shaped La Frégate café and the **Jardins de la Mer**. You'll see the towering Radisson Blu Hotel on the Waterfront to the right, and ahead a multiplex cinema, fitness centre and leisure pool. By the time you get to Albert Harbour you might feel like an evening island cruise to see the rather more lovely cliffs and beaches to the west. Nevertheless, don't miss the Harbour Gallery (https://theharbourgalleryjersey.com), Jersey's largest art and craft gallery, and the Home mural.

Boats moored at Elizabeth Marina.

Eating Out

Awabi
63 Halkett Place;
https://www.awabi.co.uk.
Named after the ormer (awabi in Japanese), this is a cool little place serving well-prepared pan-Asian dishes. It's all housed in a stylish setting which feels like a cosy wine bar. Good value, and listed in the Michelin Guide. ££

Banjo
8 Beresford Street;
www.banjojersey.com.
Part of the Jersey Pottery emporium, Banjo was converted from a former Victorian gentlemen's club and comprises a stylish brasserie and cocktail bar, along with four chic guest rooms on the second floor. Popular at weekends, so book in advance. £££

Bohemia
Green Street;
www.bohemiajersey.com.
The finest food on the island, served in the stylish surroundings of the Club Hotel and Spa, a favourite with celebrities. The chef is Steve Smith, one of the youngest chefs in the UK to achieve a Michelin Star, at the tender age of 24. He fuses tradition with innovation-producing dishes such as roasted scallops with celeriac truffle, apple, smoked eel and a truffle vinaigrette. £££

CaféJac
Jersey Arts Centre, Phillips Street;
www.cafejacco.uk.
Busy, friendly café where you can turn up any time of day for light bites or full meals. The fluffy pancakes are legendary, and there's a good choice of vegetarian dishes. It's good value and tables outside make it a popular summer choice. £

Cock and Bottle
18 Royal Street;
www.liberationgroup.com.
Traditional pub with alfresco dining on the square (heaters and blankets provided); perfect on a sunny day to enjoy classic French dishes alongside pub favourites, with chilled wine or a beer. Inside, original eighteenth-century features have been retained. ££

The Fresh Fish Company
Victoria Pier;
www.jersey.com/fresh-fish-company.
Savour a crab sandwich or lobster claw with a sea view or select fish from the retail shop to grill on a beach BBQ. The company supplies many hotels and restaurants with local fish. ££

Jeju
Fish Market;
https://www.facebook.com/jejujersey.
Named after the South Korean island, this small place serves traditional Korean and Japanese dishes using glisteningly fresh seafood from the surrounding stalls, and other local produce. £–££

Samphire
7–11 Don Street; www.samphire.je.
This is an acclaimed restaurant delivering consistently high quality cuisine in a stylish, sophisticated setting. Think foie gras with blood orange and cashew nuts or cauliflower with Romesco sauce, hazelnuts and salsa verde. £££

Tassili
Grand Jersey Hotel, The Esplanade;
https://www.handpickedhotels.co.uk/grandjersey.
Hotel restaurant noted for its stylish setting and gourmet British cuisine. Seasonal dishes are given a decadent Jersey twist. £££

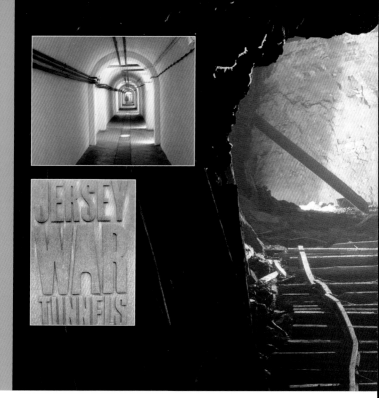

WAR TUNNELS

The preserved tunnel network brings to life the traumatic story of the five years under the Nazi Occupation.

A year after the outbreak of World War II Jersey was advertised in the UK press as "the ideal resort for wartime holidays this summer". The Jersey natives never dreamt that just a few weeks later, on 28 June 1940, Germans would be dropping bombs on their island. Within three days the island surrendered and the gruelling five-year German Occupation began.

The Channel Islands were the only territories belonging to Great Britain that fell into German hands during World War II. After the fall of France in 1940 Churchill had decided the cost of the islands' defence could not be justified and they were therefore left undefended. Hitler saw these little islands as the first step to his intended invasion of the United Kingdom. Orders were given in 1941 for Jersey to become an "impregnable fortress".

Ho8

Known as the Höhlgangsanlagen, the **Jersey War Tunnels** (Les

One of the unfinished tunnels.

into a casualty clearing station and emergency hospital. The occupying forces surrendered on 9 May 1945. Just a year later, Ho8 was opened to sightseers.

In 1961, the Royal Court ruled that the subterranean complex belonged to the private owners of the land above it, and Ho8 fell under private ownership. Now, it serves as a memorial and museum: the hospital wards have been preserved or reconstructed, and the dark, dripping tunnels maintained in their unfinished state. A combination of archive film footage, islanders' reminiscences, photos and poignant correspondence chart life under the Nazis. The exhibits bring home the hardship endured by slave labourers (at least 560 died in the Channel Islands), the deprivation of islanders and the fate of those who were deported to camps in Germany. The site also incorporates the Garden of Reflection, designed for visitors to contemplate the suffering endured during the Occupation and the historic War Trail, covering land once used as an artillery battery, and now being reclaimed by nature.

Charrières Malorey, St Lawrence; https://www.jerseywartunnels.com) was intended to be a vast network of tunnels that would serve as a barracks and protect equipment from aerial bombing. The Germans shipped in thousands of forced labourers from European nations, who were poorly fed and brutally treated. Tunnels and galleries were hewn from solid rock using gunpowder and hand tools, 50m underground. "Ho8" is one of several bunkers on the island.

The Tunnels

The complex was never completed and Ho8 did not fulfil its role. In late 1943, with the threat of an Allied invasion of Europe (Operation Overlord) becoming clear, it was decided Ho8 would be converted

Visitor Information

Jersey War Tunnels, Les Charrières Malorey, St Lawrence; www.jerseywartunnels.com.
Directions: From St Helier follow signs for A1 and The West, and keep on the A1 by branching right at the end of the Esplanade. At Bel Royal turn right onto the A11 and follow the signs for Jersey War Tunnels. Bus route No. 8 Mon–Sat all year, No. 28 from Apr–end Sep. Cycle route 4.

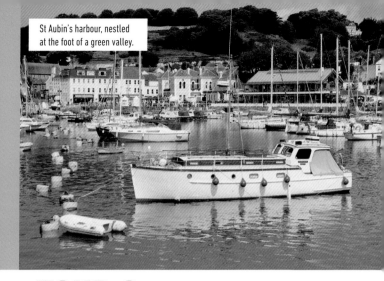

St Aubin's harbour, nestled at the foot of a green valley.

TOUR 2
The Southwest

This half-day driving or cycling tour covers 11 miles (18km) from St Aubin's Bay to Beauport, where the coast is fringed by the finest beaches on the island.

The tour follows the coast west from St Helier, via St Aubin, to the southwestern tip of the island. Cliff strolls afford fabulous views, and the choice of beach breaks ranges from big sandy bays with water sports galore to secluded little beaches sheltering below the cliffs. When it comes to restaurants you are spoilt for choice, from the quayside eateries at St Aubin to the string of cafés and fish restaurants right on St Brelade's Bay.

St Aubin's Bay

Leave St Helier via the Esplanade, following the signs for "The West" and St Aubin, keeping to the coast all the way. The gently curving, south-facing St Aubin's Bay stretches for 3 miles (5km) from Elizabeth Castle (see

Highlights

- Picturesque harbour of St Aubin
- St Brelade's Bay
- St Brelade's Parish Church and Fishermen's Chapel
- Beauport Bay

page 25) to St Aubin. The seafront promenade, formerly the route of the Western Railway Line, stretches the entire length of the bay.

During spring tides, giant waves crash over the wall here and sand bags are piled up to protect the small streets leading up from the coastal road. Normally, though, this is a calm, safe bay whose sands are lapped by the shallowest of waters. Prior

off

Reflected Glory

Halfway round St Aubin's Bay on the A1, St Matthew's Church at Millbrook is known as the Glass Church (Mon–Fri 9am–5pm and for services on Sun). The austere church walls belie a glowing interior that was decorated in opaque glass by the Art Deco glass designer René Lalique. Florence Boot (Lady Trent), the widow of Jesse Boot, founder of Boots the Chemists, commissioned Lalique to embellish the church, then dedicated it to her late husband.

The unique glass interior designed by René Lalique.

to the opening of Jersey's airport in St Peter in 1937, the sands at the eastern end of St Aubin's Bay were used at low tide for take-off and landing of seaplanes flying between the Channel Islands.

Razor fish

When the tide is very low you can have fun trying to catch razor fish (also known as razor clams) in St Aubin's Bay. Go equipped with a bag of salt, walk along the shoreline and look for the keyhole-shaped burrows in the sand. Sprinkle about a teaspoonful of salt over the hole and wait for around thirty seconds for the razor fish to pop out of its burrow. Hold the clam firmly for a few seconds while it relaxes, then pull it gently out of the hole. The fish are actually long, thin molluscs with cut-throat, razor-like shells. A slightly chewy type of clam, they are popular in parts of Europe and can be delicious if cooked correctly, ideally steamed with wine, garlic and herbs.

At Bel Royal, where the A1 and A2 converge, keep to the coast road for St Aubin's Harbour. Park just before the harbour, at the main car park on the left hand side of the road.

St Aubin

A far smaller, prettier place than St Helier, **St Aubin** ❶ lends itself to quay or seaside strolls and leisurely lunches at inviting alfresco restaurants. The first pier was built in 1675, and a small town subsequently grew up here, with the Bulwarks – the houses beside the harbour – added in 1790. Thanks to its picturesque cottages and its setting at the foot of a green valley, St Aubin was from its earliest days more popular than St Helier.

A haunt of privateers

Named after a sixth-century Breton saint, who was known as a protector against pirates, the town ironically acquired much of its wealth through

Picturesque cottages line the harbour at St Aubin.

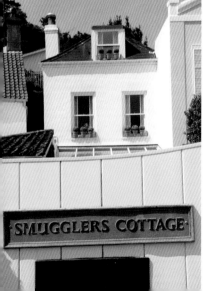

Cheers to Bergerac

To *Bergerac* fans the Old Court House in St Aubin will be familiar as the Royal Barge pub that featured in the BBC TV detective series of the 1980s. The combination of crime investigations, affluent tax exiles, beach holiday setting and Bergerac's affairs proved a huge hit, and the series ran for ten years (you can still catch up with it on some TV channels). The recently refurbished Old Court House is now a hotel with a choice of restaurants and bars.

profiteering (legalised plundering of enemy shipping), and in the seventeenth and eighteenth centuries it was the leading port on the island. During the English Civil War many a British vessel was captured and plundered by Sir George Carteret, the Royalist governor of the island. Such were the losses of British ships that Parliamentary forces were sent by Cromwell to put down the Royalist resistance.

Merchants' mansions

Merchants who grew rich on the proceeds of profiteering built themselves fine four-storey houses, often equipped with huge cellars to store the booty. Prior to the construction of the harbour, some of the Bulwarks stood right on the seashore and had spectacular roof outlooks for viewing the return of the fleet. One of the finest still standing is the **Old Court House**, overlooking the harbour, and now a hotel and restaurant. The loot was stored in the cellars and then divided in what was then the Court Room, presided over by the judges.

Fish and ships

Apart from privateering, fortunes were also made by the more

Originally a wealthy merchant's house, parts of the Old Court House Inn date back to 1450.

honourable trades of shipbuilding and cod fishing in Newfoundland. The fishing fleet used to set off across the Atlantic in springtime, returning for the harvest in autumn. The cod were dried, salted and exported, and fishing was the island's most lucrative industry until the late nineteenth century. Shipowning had also expanded rapidly, and in 1865 Jersey and Guernsey were ranked tenth in British ports. However, the islands were to suffer with the advent of iron steamships in the 1870s. These were too expensive to buy – or build – spelling the end of the great seafaring era.

Today the St Aubin vessels are either jet skis that roar around the bay, motorboats or yachts. The port is home to the **Royal Channel Islands Yacht Club** (you can see it at the end of the quayside), whose first female member was Lillie Langtry, one of

Arts and Crafts

Overlooking the port, the Harbour Gallery (The Quay, St Helier) is the largest exhibiting and selling gallery in the Channel Islands. Comprising three galleries and a textile centre, it exhibits work from over 100 local artists and craft workers, showcases a minimum of nine exhibitions a year and hosts workshops, classes and events for all ages. Wander at leisure through the galleries and choose from paintings, prints, ceramics, jewellery, woodwork and textiles. It also has an excellent little café.

Handmade local crafts for sale at the Harbour Gallery.

the most famous figures in Victorian society (see page 82). She was elected a member of the club in 1892.

The Western Railway

Overlooking St Aubin's harbour on the east side is **St Brelade's Parish Hall**, formerly the Terminus Hotel and railway station. The now defunct Western Railway, which linked St Helier to St Aubin, was extended to Corbière in 1884. Trains ran on a single line of standard-gauge track and, apart from delays caused by waves crashing over the sea wall along St Aubin's Bay, the service ran with remarkable efficiency. However, competition from buses and a fire at St Aubin's station, destroying the rolling stock, led to the demise of the service in 1936. The track was turned into a footpath and today makes a delightful 4-mile (6km) walk across the western corner of the island.

Offshore, **St Aubin's Fort ❷** was built to command the western end of the bay in the mid-16th century, predating Elizabeth Castle at St Helier.

Jersey Birds

Noirmont Point is a critical area for migrant birds; as the most southerly headland in Jersey and the last chance for birds to find food before crossing the open sea to France, it attracts large numbers. Among the less common are honey buzzard, osprey, wryneck, golden oriole, ring ouzel, shorelark, tawny pipit, ortolan and lapland bunting, barred warbler, and melodious warbler. The area was designated an ecological Site of Special Interest in 2007.

Persistent threats of invasion led to additional fortifications over the centuries, the most recent of which were built by the Germans during the Occupation in World War II. You can walk to the fort over the wet sands at low tide, but there is no access to the public as it is now used as a residential sports facility for schools and youth groups; it is only really worth visiting for the views across to St Aubin.

The underground Command Bunker gives a unique insight into German military engineering.

St Aubin's Fort was built in the 1540s to protect shipping in the bay.

Parallel to the coast road, the High Street, known also as **Rue du Crocquet**, used to be the main thoroughfare for horses and carts linking St Aubin with St Helier. Many of the houses were built by wealthy merchants at the end of the seventeenth century. Those on your right would have backed directly on to the sea, enabling vessels to load and unload. Keep going to the top of the road for fine views across the bay.

St Brelade's Parish Hall is housed in the former railway station.

Noirmont Point

Turn inland from St Aubin along the A13, which climbs up the wooded valley towards St Brelade's Bay. After about a mile (1.6km), turn left on to the B57, the Route de Noirmont, and at the small crossroads, take the left turn just beyond it for **Noirmont Point ❸**. This headland was called "Black Mount" after the clouds that gather over it – said to herald rain. A prominent relic of the Occupation is the huge underground Command Bunker of the former German coast artillery battery, complete with a large observation tower brooding on the clifftop. The bunker has been carefully restored by the Channel Islands German Occupation Society and is open to the public from April to October, most Sundays 11am–4.30pm.

The Coastal Artillery gun to the left of it originally stood at La Coupe, on the northeast coast, but after the war it was thrown over the cliffs by the British, then recovered in 1979.

Portelet Bay

Return to the junction and turn left for **Portelet Bay ❹**. Park the car at the top of the cliff, by the Old Portelet Inn and admire the views

The sand at Ouaisné Bay is perfect for making sandcastles.

from the top of the cliff. The pretty bay of Portelet below, with its soft, sheltered sands, can be reached by a long flight of steps. The beach

Portelet Bay is one of the island's most photogenic beaches.

is rarely crowded and now has the bonus of a delightful café (see page 45). The little island, accessible at low tide, is properly called the **Île au Guerdain** but more popularly known as Janvrin's Tomb, after the sea captain who was buried here.

When Janvrin was returning with his ship from plague-infested Nantes in France in 1721, he was refused entry to St Aubin's harbour for fear of contamination. Janvrin fell victim himself and, since his body was not allowed ashore, he was given a burial on the island. The body was later transferred to St Brelade's cemetery. The tower on the islet was built over the grave in 1808 as one of the many fortifications against possible invasion during the Napoleonic Wars.

Ouaisné Bay

From the Old Portelet Inn, return to the small crossroads, turn left and then take the right fork down to **Ouaisné Bay** ❺ (pronounced *Waynay*). The Old Smugglers' Inn, on le au Guerdain, home to Janvrin's Tomb.

he left as you go down, is evidence
of former activities in this corner of
the island.

The magnificent sweep of sandy
beach, sheltered between headlands,
stretches for over a mile, Ouaisné Bay
being divided from St Brelade's by a
rocky promontory called the Point
e Grouin. Even on hot days in high

season, Ouaisné's fine sandy beach has
plenty of space.

The cliffs south of the bay shelter
La Cotte de St Brelade ❻ (closed
to the public), a major archaeological
site excavated on and off for one
hundred years from 1881. Thirteen
teeth of Neanderthal man were
discovered here, along with the much
older bones of prehistoric woolly
mammoth and rhino. These piles of
bones, discovered in the 1960s and
'70s, suggested that the cave-dwellers
stampeded the animals off the cliffs to
their deaths.

Behind Ouaisné beach, the gorse-
covered common is home to some
rare species of fauna. This is the last
stronghold of the agile frog, and is
also a habitat of the Dartford warbler
and the Jersey green lizard. Sightings,
however, are rare, and visitors are
advised to keep to the pathways and
not to disturb the habitat. Protecting
Ouaisné Common from the sea and
stretching the length of the beach
is the German anti-tank wall, built
by prisoners during the German
Occupation. **Portelet Common**,
an expanse of heathland above the

Portelet Common

For dramatic sea views head for the
northern edge of Portelet Common,
a 77-acre (31-hectare) nature
reserve rising 200ft (61 metres)
above sea level. From this elevated
plateau the view takes in a huge
sweep of bay, from Ouaisné below
to the far end of St Brelade's Bay.
The habitat of gorse, dwarf shrub
heathland and lichen grassland
supports over one hundred plant
species, while the crevices of the
cliffs provide nesting and roosting
sites for shags, oystercatchers and
rock pipits.

Sweeping views of St Brelade's
Bay from Portelet Common.

The soft sand and safe bathing make sheltered, south-facing
St Brelade's one of Jersey's most popular beaches.

beach commanding splendid coastal views, can be reached by the cliff path (see box).

St Brelade's Bay

St Brelade's Bay ❼ is accessible by foot either across the sands or over the rocky promontory, depending on the tides. To reach the beach by car, return to the junction, joining the A13, then fork left on to the B66 and descend to the bay. With its gently sloping, golden sands, sheltered setting and clear, blue waters St Brelade's is justifiably the most popular beach on the island.

Above the sands, the seafront promenade is bordered by palm-fringed gardens, seafood cafés, souvenir and gift shops. The Sir Winston Churchill Park has immaculate lawns and brightly coloured flowerbeds, while on the slopes above the bay lie some highly desirable tax-exile residences, set in lush south-facing gardens.

The beach is the best equipped on the island, with sun loungers,

Seaside Treasure Trove

Design your own glass bead jewellery at Fish 'n' Beads, a quirky little beach shack on the promenade at St Brelade's Bay. There are also funky and original gifts for sale, many of them made from recycled driftwood or other finds washed up on the beach. The hut is open 10am–5pm in summer, check for times rest of year; tel: 01534-742 348.

Creative gifts from recycled driftwood.

windbreaks and a whole host of water sports: stand-up paddle boarding, kayaking, coasteering, sailing, water skiing, windsurfing and – when there are waves – surfing and bodyboarding. If you don't fancy getting wet there are plenty of beach activities including beach volleyball and beach football.

When it's time for lunch there is ample choice. You can just step straight from the sands to seafood eateries for Jersey oysters and crabs, or a laid-back café for burgers, grills or home-made cakes. The string of cafés and restaurants along the boardwalk all have tables alfresco where you can soak up the stunning sea views.

St Brelade's Church and Fisherman's Chapel

Overlooking the little port at the far end of the bay, the picturesque parish **Church of St Brelade** ❽ dates back to the twelfth century and still retains its Norman chancel.

This church was built in pink Jersey granite, and inside you can see pebbles and limpets from the beach embedded in the un-rendered walls.

Nearby, the lovely little **Fisherman's Chapel** ❾ is the oldest

place of worship on the island, built in the eleventh century on the foundations of an ancient monastic church. The chapel acquired its present name in late medieval times when it was used by the fishing guilds. Having escaped destruction during the Reformation, it was variously used as an armoury, store room and carpenter's shop. In 1880

Stroll along the Esplanade and gardens at St Brelade's.

The early-Norman Fisherman's Chapel is located beside
St Brelade's Church at the western end of the bay.

permission was finally given for
the building to revert to a church.
Restoration early in the twentieth
century brought to light the
fragments of a series of beautiful

Fragments of beautiful medieval frescoes
decorate the interior of the Fisherman's Chapel.

medieval frescoes (1375–1425),
decorating all four walls. These
were restored in 1980, and today
the scenes from the Old and New
Testaments can be made out with
the help of drawings on helpful
information boards that reconstruct
the missing outlines.

Clearest of all is the scene
depicting the *Annunciation* along
the east wall. The small kneeling
figures either side of the Virgin and
Archangel – seven males to the left
and seven females to the right – are
members of the donor's family.

The flight of granite steps linking
the churchyard with the small
harbour is the shortest **Perquage**
(sanctuary path) on the island. Before
the Reformation, criminals who
sought refuge in any of the twelve
parish churches were allowed to
escape via such paths to the safety
of a boat and sanctuary in France.
Hence each of the parishes has at least
a short section of coastline.

Beauport Bay

Take the steep road opposite the main entrance of the churchyard and turn left for **Beauport ⑩**. Reaching this unspoilt bay entails a longish trek down a bracken-clad cliff – which deters most tourists. Islanders come here, especially at weekends, when sleek yachts are often moored in the bay. There are no facilities on the beach, so take a picnic, and a sunshade or hat.

The clear, still waters are excellent for snorkelling, and children can enjoy fishing in the rock pools.

End the day at **La Corbière** (see page 46), a short drive to the west. This is a dramatic and photogenic spot to watch the sun sink into the Atlantic.

Eating Out

OUAISNÉ BAY
Kismet Cabana
Ouaisné Car Park, La Rue du Ouaisné; www.kismetcabana.com.
Street food inspired by global flavours. This laid-back shack is in Ouaisné Bay's car park but you can take away food to the beach. ££

ST AUBIN'S HARBOUR
Lazin Lizard
Mont Les Vaux; www.lazinlizard.com.
Buzzy little restaurant catering for all tastes, with dishes like Cajun-style crispy squid, Jamaican Jerk chicken, sticky ribs and steak with teriyaki prawns. ££

Salty Dog Bar and Bistro
Le Boulevard; www.saltydogbistro.com.
Relaxed alfresco dining and food that is big on flavour, freshness and spice. Cocktails and contemporary music are part of the scene. £££

ST PETER
Mark Jordan at the Beach
La Plage, La Route de la Haule; www.markjordanatthebeach.com.
Run by the same chef as the Ocean Restaurant in the Atlantic Hotel (see page 124) this casual bistro on the beachside promenade offers high quality, simple cuisine with the emphasis on fish. £££

PORTELET BAY
Portelet Bay Café
Portelet Bay; www.porteletbaycafe.com.
Family-run café right on the beach with quirky upcycled decor. Delicious wood-fired pizzas and the catch of the day is brought in by boat. A lovely scenic spot, worth the trek down from the Portelet Headland (no car access). Booking essential in summer. ££

The Old Smugglers' Inn
Le Mont de Ouaisné; www.oldsmugglersinn.com.
Popular pub, close to the beach, converted from seventeenth-century cottages. Fill up on traditional pub food beside a fire in the winter. Easy parking and the landlord is friendly. ££

ST BRELADE'S BAY
Crab Shack
La Route de la Baie; www.jerseycrabshack.com.
Rustic beachfront eatery that's all about the seafood; from home-made mackerel pâté and local crab bisque to Jersey oysters and freshly picked spider crab, all beautifully presented. ££

Oyster Box
La Route de la Baie; www.oysterbox.co.uk.
Mainly seafood restaurant with a great location on the bay. The menu stretches across the culinary spectrum from gourmet burgers to Jersey oysters, crab and lobster. Seaside terrace. ££–£££

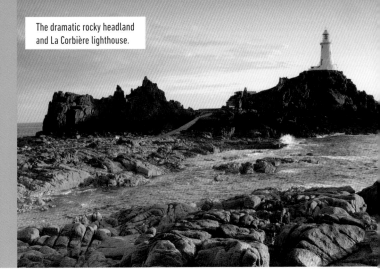

The dramatic rocky headland and La Corbière lighthouse.

TOUR 3
The West Coast

This half-day driving or cycling tour of 14 miles (22km) takes in Jersey's most dramatic coast, where surfers ride the big Atlantic swell on a spectacular 4-mile (6km) beach.

The wild and windswept bay of St Ouen's dominates the entire coast. This is a surfers' paradise, with championship-size waves and Bondi Beach-style lifeguards on patrol. On the landward side, Les Mielles is the largest remaining area of unspoilt countryside on the island, its sand-dune system rich in flora and fauna.

La Corbière

Marking the southwestern tip of the island is **La Corbière** ❶, or haunt of the crow, once considered a bird of ill omen. This is a wild and desolate corner, abounding in tales of ships that have foundered on the treacherous rocks and sailors who have drowned. The first recorded disaster on the rocks here was a Spanish vessel carrying a

> ## Highlights
> - La Corbière lighthouse
> - St Ouen's Bay
> - La Rocco
> - Channel Islands Military Museum

cargo of wine in 1495. Among the many other shipwrecks was the Royal Mail Steam Packet in 1859.

However, it was not until 1874 that a lighthouse, the first in the British Isles to be made of concrete, was built here. Perched on jagged rocks and often lashed by waves, this makes a dramatic scene at any time of day. There are still occasional accidents here, such as one involving a French catamaran, en route from Jersey to Sark, which struck a rock

Anti-Tank Walls

The 6ft (2-metre) -thick concrete wall along the entire bay of St Ouen's was one of many anti-tank walls which were built by the Germans on the Channel Islands. Orders had been given to transform the island into 'an impregnable fortress', and thousands of foreign forced labourers and Russian prisoners-of-war were imported to construct the walls, gun emplacements, artillery batteries and bunkers. Over half a million tons of concrete were used around the coasts, with narrow-gauge railways built specifically for its transport.

A World War II coastal defence gun at La Corbière.

north of the lighthouse in 1995. The sculpted pair of clasped hands on the headland commemorates the rescue of all 307 passengers and crew.

If the tide is right, you can walk across the causeway to the lighthouse, but the incoming sea is treacherous, and you should check the tides before setting out. A carved stone on the causeway recalls the fate of

The granite memorial at La Corbière pays tribute to a successful sea rescue.

an assistant lighthouse keeper who drowned while trying to save a visitor stranded by the incoming tide. Nowadays a siren warns visitors when the tide approaches the causeway.

Originally manned by four keepers, the lighthouse today is remotely operated, and there is no access inside for visitors. During World War II the Germans built bunkers at La Corbière and a great grey observation tower on the clifftop overlooking the lighthouse. This was used as a radio tower and, more recently, converted by Jersey Heritage into self-catering accommodation, in German modernist Bauhaus style. The tower is over six floors and commands a wonderful 360-degree panorama of the island from the top.

St Ouen's Bay

For **St Ouen's Bay** ❷ to the north, continue around the headland, passing above the rocky Petit Port Bay, and in about a mile (1.6km) turn left on to the B35 (if you're cycling, keep following the signs for Route 1). The longest bay in the Channel Islands, the swathe of sands stretches in a great 4-mile (6km) arc, all the

Concrete observation tower at La Corbière.

cafés above the beach with sea-view terraces. Elsewhere the beach is very exposed and not ideal for sunbathing; and when the weather is inclement, the bay is far from welcoming. All but experienced surfers should heed the danger warnings and keep to the areas between the flags where lifeguards are on duty during summer. The bay is notorious for rip tides and strong currents.

The most sheltered section is **La Pulente** in the south, where, at the right tide, children can enjoy sandy pools in the rocky outcrops.

Les Mielles

The main road skirting the bay, La Grande Route des Mielles, is also known as Five Mile Road. On foot it may feel like at least 5 miles (8km), but it is in fact less than 4 miles (6km). On the landward side, the sand dunes of **Les Mielles Conservation Zone ❸** are the habitat of a wide range of birds and plants, including several endangered species. **La Mare au Seigneur**, colloquially known as St Ouen's Pond, was, until World War II, used to stock fish for the Seigneur of St Ouen, and the reeds used for thatching and bedding. The land was purchased

way from La Pulente in the south to L'Etacq in the north. This is a beach which is never crowded.

Surfers' paradise

Throughout the year surfers make the most of the rollers on the incoming tides. Bodyboarding is hugely popular too. Surfboards, body boards, skim boards and wetsuits can be all hired at various points along the beach or, for those who prefer just to sit and watch the action, the sea wall affords shelter, and there are occasional

On the Crest of the Waves

The first stand-up surfers in Jersey were a group of South Africans who, in the 1950s, saw film footage of St Ouen's in an advertisement for the island in a UK cinema. Inspired by the bay they moved to Jersey, set up as lifeguards here and taught the islanders the art of stand-up surfing. The sport quickly caught on and the Jersey Surfboard Club – one of the oldest in Europe – was founded in 1959.

Head down to St Ouen's for guaranteed high rollers.

by the National Trust for Jersey in 1972 and is now a nature reserve. A rich diversity of flora surrounds the pond, and the nearby field called **Le Noir Pré** or 'The Orchid Field' is one of the last strongholds of the Jersey or loose-flowered orchid *(Orchis laxiflora)*, providing a blaze of colour in May and June.

The reed beds and marshy surrounds of the pond attract a large variety of birds. Since 1992, 188 species have been recorded at the site and, with changes in climate, an increasing number are arriving each year. Among the breeding birds are Cetti's warbler, reed and sedge warblers, bearded tit and reed bunting. A pair of marsh harriers bred here for the first time in 2002, and the species can often be spotted soaring overhead. The National Trust's Jersey Wetland Centre (www.nationaltrust.je/project/the-national-trust-for-jersey-wetland-centre) has panoramic views of the reed bed and pond, and is equipped with binoculars and a live-feed reed bed cam. Access is via a tunnel, entered on La Grande Route des Mielles (park at the Watersplash, cross the road, and it's just to the north).

Lewis Tower, built in 1835 to defend Jersey's coast.

A large part of the land running alongside Five Mile Road is given over to golf courses, including Les Mielles Golf and Country Club, which also has an activity centre with lots of things to entertain children, including minigolf and a fun zone.

Coastal towers

At the southern end of the bay, out to sea, **La Rocco** ❹ tower is the oldest of nine towers which were built to

La Rocco tower was badly damaged during the Occupation.

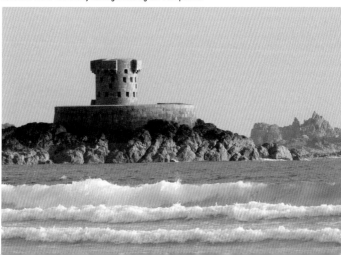

Coastline Campaign

The Coastline Campaign was set up by Jersey's National Trust to protect Jersey's wild yet vulnerable coastline. The natural environment along the west coast is one of the most important areas of natural wilderness, and much of the land is owned and managed by the National Trust. To learn more about the important work they do, join one of the regular ranger-led walks (www.nationaltrust.je).

Sea-holly can be found in the sand dunes near St Ouen's Bay.

defend the bay during the Napoleonic Wars. Damaged by German target shooting during the Occupation, the tower underwent renovation in 1969. Only three of the other towers survive, including **Kempt Tower** (1834) on the seafront further north. This is one of the few examples of a Martello tower to have survived in a good state of preservation. The ground floor was used to store weapons and armour; the upper floor housed the troops. Today the tower provides self-catering accommodation for up to twelve people.

At the north end of the bay, **Lewis Tower** stands on the site where the local rector set up a cannon in 1779, in anticipation of the capture of the island by the adventurer, the Prince of Nassau, with a French force of six thousand. The invasion was repulsed by the Jersey Militia and the French warships were forced to return to St Malo, where five of the boats were destroyed by the British. The structure you see today is a Martello tower of 1835. This was used by the Germans in World War II, who constructed an extension at the base to house a searchlight.

For centuries *vraic* (pronounced 'rack') or seaweed from the beach has been collected for use as a fertiliser on the farmland bordering the coast.

Horses and carts were once used for the job, gaining access to the beaches via slipways which you can see all the way around the Jersey coastline. In 1600 laws were passed to guarantee farmers equal rights to the free fertiliser. Today it is a free-for-all but nowadays you rarely see tractors going down to collect the vraic.

Knitting traditions

Follow La Grande Route des Mielles to the end of the main beach for the Château complex and the former **Jersey Woollen Mills**.

Seaweed is harvested in St Ouen's Bay and used as a fertiliser.

Knitting is one of the islands' oldest traditions, and records date back to the sixteenth century when women would knit sweaters to keep their menfolk warm on their long journeys to the cod banks in Newfoundland.

Jersey became famous for the trade, and knitted goods, especially stockings and waistcoats, were exported to England and France. According to the records of an early seventeenth-century Lieutenant Bailiff of Jersey, the majority of the islanders (children included) were knitters, and over ten thousand pairs of stockings were produced weekly. The noise of knitting needles during sermons became so prominent that vicars put a stop to knitting inside the church.

The harvest and *vraicing* (seaweed collection) began to suffer and in 1608, in order to encourage more workers onto the land, an act was passed prohibiting those over the age of 15 from knitting during the harvest. The penalty was imprisonment.

Each jersey made on the Channel Islands had its own distinctive style. Legend has it that if a sailor was lost at sea and his body washed ashore, he would be identified by his sweater and returned to his native parish. Sadly,

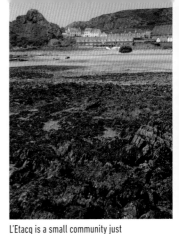

L'Etacq is a small community just a few hundred metres inland.

these days, jerseys are no longer made on the island.

Channel Islands Military Museum

A restored German bunker, sitting on the seafront next to Lewis Tower, is home to the **Channel Islands Military Museum** ❺ (www.jersey. com/things-to-do/attractions/listings/ channel-island-military-museum). The bunker is limited in space but is packed with fascinating military and civilian memorabilia from the German Occupation.

Apart from anti-aircraft guns, soldiers in uniform and military motorcycles, there is a rare Enigma decoding machine, a series of Red Cross letters to relations and friends in England and Christmas and birthday cards made by Jersey internees at the Worzach and Bieberach camps in southern Germany. Orders of the Commandant include a notice of a Jersey resident, Louis Berrier, being charged with espionage for releasing a pigeon messenger for England. He was court-martialled and executed.

Relics of Red Cross food parcels that arrived by ship towards the end of the German Occupation include tins of dried

An elegant freshwater pearl necklace on display at Jersey Pearl.

The Channel Islands Military Museum is housed in a coastal defence bunker which formed part of Hitler's Atlantic war defences.

egg. Food was severely rationed during the Occupation, but the islanders were resourceful, creating coffee from parsnips, tea from peapods and toothpaste from crushed cuttlefish and ivy.

Another tourist attraction of a different nature is **Jersey Pearl** (www.jerseypearl.com), just across the main road. In this spacious, plush showroom you can watch pearl-threading, have your own necklace made or choose from a wide range of cultured, freshwater or simulated pearls.

The main road heads inland after Jersey Pearl. The B35 takes you to **L'Etacq** ❻, a vast expanse of reefs better suited to rock pool exploring than swimming. A forest close to L'Etacq was submerged when the sea level rose after the Ice Age, and on rare occasions when the sands have been washed away by storms you can see the remains of ancient tree stumps. At the far end of the bay, and accessible by road, an old German bunker sells lobster, crabs, prawns

German Relics

Instead of destroying the conspicuous evidence of an unhappy episode in its history, Jersey retained its German relics after World War II. Apart from becoming tourist attractions, they have been put to good use. The sea wall along St Ouen acts as a barrier against the Atlantic, one of the bunkers is home to the Channel Islands Military Museum, another a restaurant and retail outlet for freshly caught lobsters, while the six-storey, sea-view observation tower at Corbière has been converted for holiday lets.

A World War II German pistol displayed in the Channel Islands Military Museum.

Faulkner Fisheries in L'Etacq, at the northern end of St Ouen's Bay, supply many major Jersey restaurants with fresh seafood.

and fresh fish. For a gourmet picnic, order ready-cooked lobster (Faulkner Fisheries; www.faulknerfisheries.com) or enjoy delicious and affordable barbecued seafood at wooden benches overlooking the coast. Don't be put off by the occasional bad odour on the coast here – it's only accumulated weed from Le Pulec to the north – familiarly known as Stinky Beach.

To enjoy some spectacular views from castle ruins you could head on north up to **Grosnez** (see page 78) on the north coast – a diversion of approximately 3 miles (5km). Otherwise retrace your steps along the B35 and join the B64 to reach the village of **St Ouen**.

The **parish church of St Ouen** ❼ is one of the finest on the island, and lies southwest of the actual village, on the crest of a hill overlooking the sea. To get there take the A12, then the C117 marked to the right. Notably, the church was mentioned in a charter signed by William the Conqueror prior to his conquest of England. Major alterations and extensions took place between the twelfth and nineteenth centuries. The original building, possibly a chantry chapel erected by a group of monks from Normandy in the seventh century, is thought to have been rebuilt or enlarged by a member of the historic de Carteret family, Seigneurs of St Ouen, whose nearby ancient seat can be seen from the main A12.

The magnificent **Manor of St Ouen** ❽ (closed to the public), owned by the family for more than 800 years, was used by the German army during the Occupation. Inside the grounds, the Chapel of St Anne, built at the same time as the manor, was turned into a storeroom and butcher's shop. The manor is now a popular wedding venue.

aMaizin!

At La Houge Farm, St Peter, Jersey's aMaizin! Adventure Park (www.jersey leisure.com) has ample to entertain the kids: a toboggan run, pedal-karts, tractor rides, hands-on craft activities, an indoor fun zone with soft play area, animals and, in July and August, a maze constructed entirely of the cereal crop. If you prefer to see where you're going, visit in early July before the maze gets too high. In September the crop is cut down and passed to a local farmer for feed.

The next village along the A12 is **St Peter's**, whose parish church has the tallest spire on the island and so flashes a warning red light for planes landing and taking off from the nearby airport. A church has stood on this site for over one thousand years, like St Ouen's, pre-dating the Conquest. It has some unusual stained glass windows, including one about the airport.

Return to St Helier by continuing south along the A12 and turning left on to the A1 when you come to the main junction.

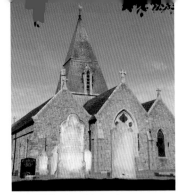

Parts of St Ouen's parish church may predate 1066.

Eating Out

ST OUEN'S BAY
El Tico Beach Cantina
La Grande Route des Mielles; www.elticojersey.com.
A familiar landmark of St Ouen's Bay, and a favourite surfers' haunt. The original café here dated back to 1948 but was rebuilt in Art Deco style. Open for breakfast, lunch and dinner, with plenty of vege options, it's also a surf school and is a great spot to watch the waves roll in. ££

Faulkner Fisheries
La Grande Route des Havres; www.faulknerfisheries.com.
Faulkner Fisheries' Summer BBQ turns out freshly grilled seafood served at simple tables overlooking the beach, beside their shop housed in a WW2 bunker at L'Etacq. Expect the likes of seared local scallops, grilled lobster or fish of the day, and a vegetarian dish. Weather dependent. ££

Le Braye
La Grande Route des Mielles; www.lebraye.com.
Gaze across the huge bay of St Ouen's and stoke up on big breakfasts before hitting the waves. Or come for crustaceans, Jersey beef or falafel burgers or Jersey cream teas. This is one of the safer areas for swimming at St Ouen's so it's very popular with families. ££

Ocean Restaurant
Atlantic Hotel, La Mont de la Pulente; www.theatlantichotel.com.
Enjoy sublime views of St Ouen's Bay in a chic blue and white room, while eating award-winning cuisine based on the finest Jersey produce. Breakfast, lunch and dinner daily. £££

Sands
La Grande Route des Mielles; http://sands-cafe.co.uk.
Formerly known as Big Vern's and overlooking the rollers of St Ouen's Bay, this is the favourite restaurant of local surfers and a great spot for brunch. Choose from fourteen-hour slow cooked pork tacos, breakfast burritos, burgers, sandwiches and several vegetarian options. ££

Watersplash Beach & Bar Diner
La Grande Route Des Mielles; www.watersplashjersey.com.
With gorgeous views of the bay and a laid back vibe, Watersplash is open for breakfast, light bites and main meals with plenty of vege options, as well as drinks at the bar. £–££

FABLES AND FESTIVALS

Jersey abounds with myth, superstition and strange customs. Prehistoric menhirs and dolmens gave rise to devil worship and witchcraft, and stormy seas sowed the seeds of legend.

Many are the tales of wreckers who lured ships onto the treacherous reef of La Corbière by burning fires near the rocks, indicating a safe haven from the stormy waters. The invariable shipwreck would bring death to the crew and precious cargo to the fishermen.

Medieval legend tells the story of the dragon of St Lawrence, who terrorised the islanders and who was slain by Lord of Hambye from Normandy.

On the north coast tales were told of the *Black Dog of Bouley Bay*, a terrifying creature with huge saucer eyes that roamed the coastline of the bay.

Some islanders are still superstitious. Legend has it that anyone who witnesses cattle on bended knees on Christmas Eve (in other words, worshipping) will die before the year is out. Several of the old farmers still make sure their cattle are bedded well before the midnight hour.

Among Jersey's ancient customs is *les visites du branchage*, the twice-yearly inspections by parish officials to check

Jersey International Air Display.

– all accompanying the parade of spectacular floral floats. Competition between the parishes is fierce.

Festivals and Events

For full listings go to www.jersey.com.

Walking Through Spring Festival: April. Walking festival organised by the National Trust for Jersey.

Liberation Day: 9 May. Islanders celebrate the liberation from the German forces on 9 May 1945.

La Fête du R'nouvé: May. Boutique festival with acoustic music, traditional dance, crafts and storytelling at La Hougue Bie.

13th Parish Festival of Independent Films and Music: May. International short films and documentaries.

June in Bloom: end June. Colourful floral festival with tours, talks and workshops.

Battle of Flowers: Grand Parade second Friday in August, followed on Saturday by the Illuminated Moonlight Parade, with selected floats and bands.

Gorey Fête: Friday of third week in August. Beach events, fairground rides.

Jersey International Air Display: mid-September.

CI Pride: mid-September. The Channel Islands' biggest and most vibrant LGBTQ+ parade, held on Jersey and Guernsey.

Tennerfest: October/ November. Dining from £10 at over 100 restaurants.

Delicious Dine-Out Festival: October to mid-November. Menus and dishes which champion local produce, at restaurants across the island.

International Guitar Festival: November.

La Fête de Noué: December. Christmas festival. Street entertainment, parades and markets in St Helier.

that no boughs or bushes encroach on roads and footpaths. Fines can be levied on landowners who fail to keep their hedges in trim.

Battle of Flowers

Of all Jersey's festivals, the biggest crowd-puller is the **Battle of Flowers**. The first "Battle" took place in 1902 on Victoria Avenue, St Helier, to celebrate the Coronation of King Edward VII. With the exception of World War I and the German Occupation, the event has been held here every year since. Formerly the flowers were ripped out of the floats and a real battle of flowers ensued. Nowadays the entertainment is provided by marching bands, dancers, beauty queens headed by Miss Jersey and a celebrity Mr Battle

Spectacular swathes of lavender at Jersey Lavender Farm.

TOUR 4

Flowers and Farming

Full of botanical and rural delights, this whole-day driving or cycling tour of 14 miles (22km) takes you to a heritage museum, vineyards, watermills and a fragrant lavender farm.

Away from the coast you'll find a surprisingly unspoilt landscape of valleys, woods, country lanes and farming land. Agriculture is no longer a main source of income for Jersey, but farming is still a way of life for at least some of the islanders. Half of the land is agricultural, and the sunny south-facing slopes yield Jersey Royal potatoes and tomatoes, while the famous Jersey cow provides islanders with milk, cream and butter.

The temperate climate, long hours of sunshine and rich soil make Jersey a gardener's paradise. Each year the island puts on a programme of open gardens, demonstrations, flower shows and environmental walks. Flowers are grown both for export and for the decoration of floats at Jersey's celebrated Battle of Flowers. The island is also famous for

Highlights
- Waterworks Valley
- Hamptonne Country Life Museum
- Tour and tastings at La Mare Wine Estate
- Jersey Lavender

its orchids, both wild and cultivated, as well as other species of rare wildflowers. During the August summer flower show the **Royal Jersey Agricultural and Horticultural Society** (www.royaljersey.co.uk) arranges four shows a year (in March, June, August and October) with some spectacular floral and vegetable displays.

Owners of private gardens occasionally open their gates to the

Hedge Veg

When you're driving along the lanes inland you may come across fresh produce (especially Jersey Royals) sold at roadside stalls outside farms and private houses. You choose what you want and leave the correct change in an honesty box. You used to see them everywhere but now many have been replaced by the growing number of farm shops.

Cash and carry along the country lanes.

public on Sundays at other times of year. For information visit www.jersey.com.

Battle of Flowers

From St Helier, follow the signs for 'The West' and the A1, taking you along the Esplanade. This becomes Victoria Avenue, venue of the annual Battle of Flowers which takes place every August and features bands, celebrities and a long parade of spectacular floats made of flowers. Tickets can be purchased online at www.battleofflowers.com.

Apart from breaks during World War I and the German Occupation in World War II, the event has taken place every year since 1902, when the first 'Battle' celebrated the Coronation of King Edward VII. It is one of the largest floral carnivals in Europe.

The cluster of faithfully restored buildings at Hamptonne Country Life Museum capture the spirit of rural Jersey.

A day or two before the event volunteers can be seen busily cutting blooms and gluing them to the floats, though these days many are made of paper. If you happen to miss the Battle of Flowers, some of these amazing creations can be seen displayed around the parishes for a few days following the event.

Before the 1960s it really *was* a battle, with floats being stripped

A goodwyf *gives you the latest seventeenth-century farming gossip.*

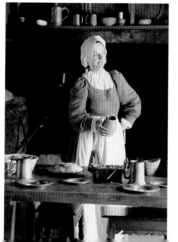

and both participants and onlookers pelting each other with flowers. Nowadays the floats remain intact, and it's more about marching bands and beauty queens. The event takes place on the second Friday in August, with an illuminated Moonlight Parade the Saturday evening after.

Waterworks Valley

When the road divides, follow signs for the A1 which take you along the inner coastal road. Keep to this road until you see a turning to the right with a small sign for **Waterworks Valley ❶** (C118). The road twists up through the lush green valley. This is one of Jersey's loveliest natural features, with leafy glades and woodland paths. The stream here used to power six watermills – hence the original name of the road, 'Le Chemin des Moulins'. The late nineteenth century saw the construction of the 3-mile (5km) long Millbrook reservoir, followed later by the Dannemarche and Handois reservoirs to the north, giving the valley its somewhat pedestrian name.

Traditional apple press in the cider barn at Hamptonne.

Hamptonne Country Life Museum

Beyond the Dannemarche Reservoir, fork left (on the C119) to get to the **Hamptonne Country Life Museum ❷** (La Rue de la Patente; www.jerseyheritage.org), which is tucked away in a lovely rustic setting, surrounded by gardens, meadows and woodland.

The group of farmhouses and outbuildings of this 15th century farm have been restored to demonstrate several hundred years of the island's rural heritage. Named after their former owners, the Langlois, Hamptonne and Syvret families, the interiors have been renovated as the homes of farming families of the seventeenth and eighteenth centuries.Syvret House gives an insight into 1940s rural life including farming traditions, day-to-day family life, language, religion and the German Occupation.

The nearby cider barn *(pressoir)* houses the apple crusher and twin-screw apple press that are still used every autumn to make cider. During La Fais'sie d'Cidre (Cider Festival) in mid-October you can see the cider being made in the old-fashioned way, with a horse crushing the apples and the juice then extracted on the press.

This is very much a living museum, often with a farmer's wife *(goodwyf* in the Jersey patois) in period costume to tell you tales of the English Civil War or the latest gossip from the seventeenth-century farming

TOUR 4   HAMPTONNE COUNTRY LIFE MUSEUM

Pallot Museum

This fascinating collection of steam and farm machinery, motor vehicles, vintage bikes and organs was put together by the late Don Pallot, a talented Jersey engineer. He invented farming implements to facilitate life for Jersey farmers, among them the Pallot Elevator Digger and the Last Furrow Reversible Plough. On Thursdays you can travel in a Victorian steam-drawn coach. (Located east of Hamptonne, off the A9 on Rue du Bechet, Trinity; www.pallotmuseum.co.uk; bus route No 5 stops nearby).

A Jersey builder's truck; a 1931 Chevrolet 30 cwt lorry.

community; or you might find a spinner or lace-maker demonstrating bygone skills. Youngsters can follow a nature trail, meet the Hamptonne piglets and calves or test their knowledge with activity sheets or puzzles in the Children's Room.

Make sure you stop at the Hamptonne Café, which serves freshly-made cakes and snacks.

La Mare Wine Estate

Continue along the B39 as far as St Mary's Village and then follow the signs along the C103 towards the Devil's Hole and **La Mare Wine Estate ❸** (www.lamarewineestate. com). From a small vineyard La Mare has grown into one of Jersey's main tourist attractions, as well as a wedding and corporate venue. The 25-acre (10-hectare) wine estate produces red, white, rosé and sparkling wines as well as apple brandy, and Jersey gin and vodka made from Jersey Royals. Guided tours of the vineyards, winery,

distillery and chocolate kitchen include tastings along the way.

The sparkling wines are made according to the *méthode champenoise* – Jersey is on the same degree of latitude as Champagne; they also make a sparkling cider, apple brandy, along with jams, marmalades, jellies and Jersey black butter (a type of preserve, not a butter).

If you don't make it to La Mare itself you can always purchase their products from the Maison La Mare in King Street, St Helier, or order them online.

St Peter's Valley

Return to St Mary's Village and take the B26, signed to **St Peter's Valley**. This will eventually join the A11, which continues through this lovely green valley – it was here that Queen Victoria was brought when she asked to see the most beautiful spot on the island. The valley was the site of six watermills, used mainly for grinding flour.

Daily guided tours with tastings will take you through the vineyards, orchards and distillery of La Mare Wine Estate.

Jersey cows in St Peter's Valley.

Turn right on to the B58, just over a mile along the A11, to see the only surviving fully working water mill on the island, the **Moulin de Quétivel ❹** (Mont Fallu; www.nationaltrust.je). A mill has operated here intermittently

A sparkling wine selection from La Mare Wine Estate.

since feudal times, the current one dating from the eighteenth century. Abandoned in the early twentieth century, it was revived by the Germans during the Occupation, only to fall into disrepair again and be further damaged by fire in 1969. It was eventually brought back to working order and beautifully restored by the National Trust in 1979.

The top floor has an exhibition on the history of milling, while the first and ground floors demonstrate how the mill works. There is a shop selling freshly ground organic flours and a wide range of locally produced gifts and a film showing how cabbage loaves (still sold in some bakeries on the island) are made in gorse ovens.

You can take the footpath from the mill to the mill pond, through red squirrel-inhabited woodland, or follow another path to Tesson Mill, and to the beach beyond this.

Le Moulin de Tesson (Tesson Mill), at the entrance to St Peter's Valley, has also been restored by the National Trust. There has probably

St. Brelade has free-draining soil and a mild climate, providing the perfect growing conditions for lavender.

been a mill on the site since the eleventh century. To fund the restoration of the waterwheel and steam-engine room the National

Moulin de Quétivel is the only working mill left in St Peter's Valley, and still grinds its own flour.

Trust had to grant a long lease to convert the interior to residential apartments. A short film relates the history of the mill. The site was temporarily closed recently for archaeological surveys.

Jersey Lavender

Continuing on the B58, go straight over the next crossroads for the A12. Turn left here and right at the roundabout which bypasses the airport and brings you into St Brelade. Just after the Quennevais shopping precinct turn left along the B25, signposted to **Jersey Lavender** ❺ (www.jerseylavender.co.uk). The fields of lavender, covering 9 acres (4 hectares), provide a Provence-like blaze of purple throughout the summer. This is a family-owned and -run business that was set up in the 1980s. The garden contains around sixty different varieties of lavender, plus dozens of culinary, medicinal, aromatic and dyers' herbs. The lavender is cut by hand, distilled on site and the essential oils matured and blended with other ingredients

For plant-lovers, there are over sixty varieties of lavender on view at Jersey Lavender, and most are for sale.

to produce eau de toilette, colognes, soap, lotions and lavender bags. You can join a guided tour of the farm, where all the different stages of harvesting and production are explained, and there are also audio tours, and talks about the distillation process.

The best time to visit is late May/early June to late July/early August – the *lavandage* or lavender harvest is usually over by early-August, but visitors can still watch the distilling and bottling processes and purchase products made from the lavender essence. Further attractions are the herb garden, nature trail and Sprigs Café (see page 67) where lavender

Jersey National Trust

If you're a member of the National Trust, make sure you take your card when you go to Jersey. The island has its own National Trust (www.nationaltrust.je) dedicated to preserving sites of historic, aesthetic and natural interest. It is the largest private landowner on Jersey, maintaining over 170 sites. Admission to the sites is free for NT members on production of a membership card. The organisation has a year-round programme of free, themed guided walks; collect a leaflet from the National Trust office at The Elms, La Chève Rue, in St Mary for further details.

The Jersey National Trust was founded in 1936.

Judith Querée's Garden

Plant enthusiasts should not miss an opportunity to take a tour of Judith Querée's Garden, set in a peaceful valley in the parish of St Ouen and encircling a 350-year-old traditional Jersey granite cottage. It is only just over 0.25 acres (0.1 hectares) in size but it manages to pack in around two thousand (mainly herbaceous) perennials from all over the world, many of them rare and unusual. Judith gives personal guided group tours of her award-winning garden by appointment. The full address is: Creux Baillot Cottage, Le Chemin des Garennes, Leoville; www.judithqueree.com. Not suitable for young children.

The late Eric Young devoted his life to breeding new hybrids of orchid, and his exhibitions won prestigious awards. He first established a collection in Jersey in 1958, and within a decade it was recognised as one of the leading private collections in Europe and multiple times winner of the Chelsea Flower Show Gold Award. Young's ambition to set up an orchid foundation open to the public was achieved, but he died in 1984 at the age of 73, before the project was completed.

The fruits of his lifelong efforts can be seen in the growing houses where exotic orchids of dazzling colours are set against a backdrop of ponds, branches, rocks and raised beds.

There is a dazzling display of orchids on show at the Eric Young Orchid Foundation.

finds its way into a number of sweet and savoury dishes.

To return to St Helier take the B25 eastwards and join the main coastal road back to St Helier.

Detour to Eric Young Orchid Foundation

Floral enthusiasts should not leave Jersey without a visit to the **Eric Young Orchid Foundation** ❻ (Victoria Village; http://ericyoung orchid.org), tucked away in the heart of the countryside in the parish of Trinity. From St Helier take the ring road, following signs to 'The North', then turn off for the A8 to Trinity. After half a mile, turn right, following signposts for Les Grands Vaux and the Orchid Foundation. The road takes you past Les Grands Vaux reservoir, then to Victoria Village, where the Foundation is signposted to the left.

Immerse yourself in exotic orchid blooms at the Eric Young Orchid Foundation.

Eating Out

ST AUBIN'S BAY
The Lookout

First Tower, Victoria Avenue; https://thelookoutjersey.com. Between St Helier and St Aubin, with views across the bay of St Aubin, this beachside restaurant has a good range of options for breakfast, brunch, lunch or dinner, from the likes of sourdough crumpets with smashed avocado, htumous, poached egg and smoked salmon, to burgers and seafood, with plenty of salads and vegetarian and vegan choices. £–££

ST MARY
Vineyard Café

La Mare Wine Estate; www.lamarewineestate.com. Look out on to neat rows of vines and enjoy light lunches or Jersey cream teas with home-made jams from the estate. ££

ST PETER'S VALLEY
The Victoria

La Vallée de St Pierre, near Moulin de Quétival; https://thevictoria.je. Colloquially known as the Vic in the Valley, this is a friendly pub with draught and cask ales, reasonably priced pub grub, alfresco seating with garden views and log fires in winter. £–££

ST BRELADE
Off The Rails

Petite route des Mielles; www.offtherailsjersey.com. Situated in the Elephant Park, Off The Rails serves authentic sourdough pizza and tapas as well as a – few summer specials and cocktails. £££

Sprigs Café

Jersey Lavender Farm, Rue du Pont Marquet; https://jerseylavender.co.uk. Light lunches and a range of home-made cakes and scones. £

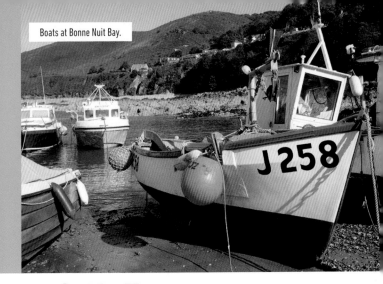

Boats at Bonne Nuit Bay.

TOUR 5
The North Coast

No visit to Jersey is complete without a tour of the dramatic northern coastline, where flower-clad cliffs tower over beautiful bays. Take this 22-mile (35km) whole-day tour by car or bike.

Allow a whole day for all the diversions, take a picnic lunch or stop for a bite of freshly caught seafood. The pretty bay of **Bonne Nuit**, with a beach, car park and excellent café, makes an ideal place for a break.

The majestic cliffs of the north extend along the entire coast, affording spectacular views across to the other Channel Islands and France.

Dotting the shore are half a dozen little bays, with fishing ports sheltered by rocky headlands. Each of these links up with the north coast footpath, which runs all the way from **Rozel** in the east to **Grosnez** in the west.

Try to cover at least a small section of this glorious coastline on foot. Choose a clear day so you can enjoy the views – and preferably when there's not a

Highlights
- Rozel Bay
- Bonne Nuit Bay
- Devil's Hole
- Bay and Barracks of Grève de Lecq
- Plémont beach and café
- Medieval ruins of Grosnez Castle

north or easterly wind. Don't forget to bring binoculars for spotting the birds that have habitats in the crevices and rocky outcrops. Species you are likely to see are fulmars, cormorants and shags, and – if you happen to be at Plémont in the spring, you might spy a puffin. Dolphins, grey seals and basking sharks are also occasionally seen from the cliff paths. Cycle route #1 follows the north

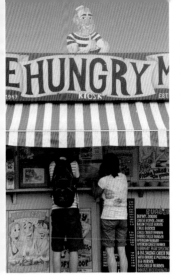

Stop for a crab sandwich at the Hungry Man kiosk in Rozel Bay.

coast from Rozel Bay right across to Les Landes.

Rozel

From the St Helier ring road follow signs for 'The North' and the Five Oaks roundabout. From here take the A6 to St Martin's, then follow the B38 up to **Rozel Bay ❶**.

Tucked away in the northeast corner of the island, this is a small, picturesque creek where fishermen's houses overlook the tiny harbour and the sand and shingle beach. The pier was built in 1829, during the heyday of the oyster industry, when there were around 30 oyster fishing vessels based in the small port. Beside the pier you're unlikely to miss the legendary Hungry Man kiosk, famous for its fabulous crab sandwiches.

Being the closest point in Jersey to France, at the height of the Napoleonic threat Rozel was considered a valuable defence site. However, no shot was ever fired here in battle.

The lush **Rozel Valley**, tucked away behind the village, makes a pleasant inland walk with its exotic trees and shrubs. Subtropical flora were first planted here by a 19th-century naturalist, Samuel Curtis, and some of them can still be seen today. The Château la Chaire Hotel has a lovely valley setting and offers fine dining in an oak-panelled restaurant or lighter fare and afternoon tea in the conservatory brasserie.

Bouley Bay

Head westwards out of Rozel on the C93 and after 1.2 miles (2km) turn right into the Rue du Bouillons (C95). At the next junction turn right and from here follow signs for **Bouley Bay ❷**. As you near the coast the road snakes its way down through the wooded hillside to a pebble bay surrounded by high cliffs. The steeply shelving beach and the deepest waters around the island's shores are ideal for scuba-diving or snorkelling. The sea here is rich in marine life, including lobsters, crabs, sea urchins and starfish, along with many species of fish.

Wander off the beaten track into St Catherine's Wood, otherwise known as Rozel Woods.

Bouley Bay and the fort of L'Etacquerel.

The **Bouley Bay Dive Centre,** based below the Water's Edge Chalets, offers lessons and facilities to divers of all standards, including 'try dives' for complete beginners. Bouley Bay is also the venue of the very popular Hillclimbs, which take place up the steep and twisty road from the bay four times a year.

Any member of the Jersey Motor Cycle and Light Car Club equipped with motorbike, saloon car, racing car, sports car or even a bike is welcome to participate. The village is otherwise peaceful, with no more to it than the hotel and a café above the beach.

Fort L'Etacquerel and Fort Leicester

On the east side of the bay, perched above the sea, the fort of **L'Etacquerel ❸** was one of several defences built to guard the north coast from French invaders. Another was **Fort Leicester** to the west of the bay, reached up the steps to the left just before the jetty. Both forts have been converted into holiday accommodation by Jersey Heritage, L'Etacquerel providing 'stone tent' accommodation for 10 with sleeping bags, Fort Leicester a relatively comfortable sea-view retreat for up to eight people. Cliff paths either side of Bouley Bay provide delightful walks. In summer the hills are ablaze with heather and wildflowers, while shags, which nest in cliff crevices in the spring, can be seen flying close to the shore.

The Black Dog of Bouley Bay.

Bonne Nuit

Leaving Bouley Bay, climb back up to the top of the hill and turn right at the T-junction along the Rue de la Petite Falaise (C96). In less than half a mile turn right to join the main A8. Take the next main right turn (B63) and follow the signs for Bonne Nuit.

To the right **Les Platons**, at 420ft (133 metres) above sea level, is the highest spot in Jersey – hence the forest of TV and radio masts. The deep cave at **Belle Hougue Point**, where the remains of prehistoric deer were discovered, lies below. Only experienced climbers, with ropes, should contemplate attempting the descent.

The name **Bonne Nuit ❹** (Good Night) appears to have derived from the now non-existent Chapel of Bona Nochte, built in the twelfth century. Conversely, the sea beyond the bay used to be called Maurepos (Bad Repose), possibly on account of smugglers.

Black Dog of Bouley Bay

During the latter half of the 18th century numerous tales were told of the Black Dog of Bouley Bay, a huge beast which roamed the cliffs around the bay, dragging its chain behind it. The dog would terrify victims by circling them with the chain, leaving them unharmed but in a state of shock. Any rumour of the Black Dog roaming the region and the locals would hot-foot it home. The stories are believed to have been the invention of smugglers – of whom there were many at the time – to frighten prying parishioners away from the bay and leave the coast clear to land their cargoes of spirits and tobacco.

Secluded Bonne Nuit Bay was a prime spot for smuggling in the seventeenth and eighteenth centuries; its pier is now the finishing point for an annual rowing race.

Today it is a secluded little bay, with a tiny harbour and a sand and shingle beach, sheltered below heather-clad hills. At low tide fishing boats and pleasure cruisers are beached on the sands, and resident mallard ducks waddle across the bay, hoping for a crust or two from the Bonne Nuit Beach Café (see page 81).

The red wooden huts on the jetty belong to fishermen who go out daily for lobsters, crabs and clams. In ancient times fishermen and other islanders rowed around Le Cheval Guillaume or Cheval Roc, the offshore rock, to protect them from evil spirits. Bonne Nuit pier is the finishing point for the Sark to Jersey Rowing Race, held either in June or July depending on the tides, and a plaque, unveiled by Chay Blyth (who, with John Ridgeway, rowed the Atlantic in 92 days in 1966) commemorates the silver jubilee. The fastest rowers from Sark take about 2.5 hours.

Sorel Point

As you head northwest you will see a sign to Sorel Point, which is the most northerly tip of the island, commanding magnificent sea views. Weather permitting, you can make out the islands of Alderney, Guernsey, Sark, the coast of Normandy and the Paternoster Reef closer to shore. Keep your eyes focused out to sea and make sure to avoid the views to the east – Ronez Quarry is one of the very few blots on the north coast landscape.

Solitary Sorel Point.

The soft wool of the Manx Loagthan sheep is prized by weavers.

Keep the Sheep

As part of a project to help restore Jersey's coastal grasslands and heath, the National Trust introduced a herd of multi-horned Manx Loagthan sheep to the Mourier Valley between Sorel Point and Devil's Hole. These spectacular sheep have an average of four horns (but have been known to grow up to seven!), love brambles, gorse and nettles and are the closest living breed to the now extinct multi-horned Jersey sheep that used to graze here over two hundred years ago.

La Crête Fort

On the promontory to the east of the bay **La Crête Fort** ❺ was built by the British in 1835, on a site that was first militarised in the sixteenth century. The fort was extended during the German Occupation in World War II, and was later used by the Lieutenant-Governor as a weekend retreat. Jersey Heritage has renovated the fort for holiday lets. Tenants can enjoy spectacular sea views to Guernsey, Sark and France, and there's a secluded beach close by.

Take the C99 out of Bonne Nuit, going westwards and when you arrive at the T-junction turn right on to the B52. This will take you to the village of St John's where you turn right on to the main A9. After the church take another right turn, on to the C101, which merges into the C100.

Resident mallard ducks patrol the beach at Bonne Nuit Bay.

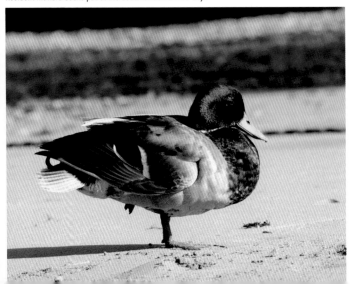

Devil's Hole

The main road veers away from the coast and becomes a Green Lane (with a speed limit of 15mph/24kmh). At the next crossroads turn right for Le Creux du Vis (Screw Hole) or, as it is more popularly known, **Devil's Hole** ❻. Park at the Priory Inn and take the steep footpath down the hill to see this spectacular natural feature, a great blowhole, created by a collapsed cave.

The melodramatic name is thought to have derived from the figurehead of a mid-nineteenth-century French shipwreck, which was washed up in the Devil's Hole and crafted into a wooden horned devil. Over the years various replicas of the devil have been placed on the path going down to add atmosphere, but each one has been stolen. Keep an eye out for the latest one.

The land is owned by the Jersey National Trust, which was responsible for the work carried out at the site to provide safer access for visitors. Wooden steps have been replaced by a tarmac path with handrails leading to a viewing platform, telescope and

The sea flows into the spectacular Devil's Hole.

interpretation panels, and a further decked platform offers sight of the Devil's Hole and the waters crashing as the tide comes up.

Grève de Lecq

From Devil's Hole follow the road south towards the village of St Mary,

Cliffs and rocky headlands protect the intimate, sandy beach at Grève de Lecq – the north coast's most popular and busiest family beach.

La Mare Wine Estate

Going south from Devil's Hole, you may want to check out all the Jersey specialities at La Mare Wine Estate (see page 62). You're unlikely to have time for a guided tour and tasting of the winery, but you can get access to the shop (and café) without having to pay the admission fee. The shop has a tempting selection of sparkling and still wines, liqueurs, chocolates and a whole range of preserves – all made at La Mare.

Chocolate heaven at La Mare Wine Estate gift shop.

and take the signs for Grève de Lecq. In the 1860s a decision was made to create a safe harbour for boats from the island's large fishing fleet. But this never came about. The original pier, started in 1872, was poorly constructed and almost entirely demolished by storms. It lay in ruins for years, and it was not until the following century that it was finally made safe – as a truncated little jetty.

Today **Grève de Lecq** ❼ is a popular beach resort, drawing far more visitors than any of the other north coast bays. It offers ample parking, easy access, a sandy beach, a pub and guesthouse (the Prince of Wales) and a couple of cafés. Children and ducks enjoy the sands here and fishermen cast their lines from the jetty. Overlooking the bay to the east and reached along the coastal path, **Le Câtel de Lecq** (Lecq Castle) is said to have been the site of an Iron Age hill fort.

The old pier at Grève de Lecq is an excellent vantage point for budding young anglers.

Behind the beach, the National Trust for Jersey has restored the Grève de Lecq barracks from the Napoleonic Wars.

Grève de Lecq Barracks

Standing behind the bay, the **Grève de Lecq Barracks** were built to house garrison troops in 1810 when the island feared a French invasion, and are the only surviving barracks on the north coast. Restored by the National Trust, the barracks are today home to the North Coast Visitors' Centre, devoted to the wildlife and history of the area, plus history and military exhibits and a collection of horse-drawn carriages. The officers' quarters at the Barracks have been converted into holiday lets.

Le Moulin de Lecq

Further back along the main road, **Le Moulin de Lecq**, which has been converted into an inn, was formerly a flour-grinding watermill. It dates from the fourteenth century, was used for over six hundred years and still retains its massive mill wheel. The stream here, which gushes out on to the beach, is the dividing line between the parishes of St Mary and St Ouen.

Plémont

The last beach on the north coast is **Plémont ❽**, or more correctly La Grève au Lançon (Sand-Eel Beach). To get there, take the road out of Grève de Lecq (the B65), turning right on to the B55, and right again at the small crossroads at Portinfer. Plémont beach to the north remains unspoilt thanks largely to the lack of vehicular access.

Leave the car at the park above the bay and walk down the cliff path then

Refreshments await you at Le Moulin de Lecq inn.

Jersey Puffins

Atlantic puffins inhabit the northwest corner of Jersey nesting in the cliffs from Plémont east to Grand Becquet. Puffins lay only one egg per year, and the decline in numbers is of great concern – in 2022 there were just four breeding pairs left on the island. The causes of the decline are not clear, but marine traffic along with predators and disturbance by humans are probably all factors. A seabird protection zone has been established here to try to enhance breeding success, and two giant puffin sculptures were unveiled in 2022 to raise awareness. The least intrusive place to try and see the birds is from the footpath between Plemont and Greve de Lecq.

headland to the east, accessible by the north coast footpath, is a good place for birdwatching, especially in late spring/ summer. The cliffs here have been home to a colony of puffins for over one hundred years (see box).

In 2015 Jersey residents heaved a sigh of relief when it was announced that the beautiful headland above Plémont Bay would be restored to its natural state. For years the site of a derelict Pontins holiday camp, it was purchased by a commercial company who threatened to build a large development here. The National Trust successfully campaigned against the project and after a hearing in Jersey's Royal Court, and with help from the States of Jersey, the park was sold to the trust in a multi-million deal. The campsite was demolished and archaeologists began examining the area.

Les Landes

take the long flight of steps that leads from the café down to the beach. Low tide reveals a wide expanse of fine sands, rock pools and a network of caves in the cliffs on the landward side; but at high tide there is no sand to be seen. The

Returning to Portinfer, rejoin the B55 going westwards. Take the next turning to the right, a narrow road signed to **Les Landes Race Course**, which lies to the left as you head towards the cliffs.

Le Moulin de Lecq, now a public house, was one of the many ancient watermills of the island.

Walk This Way

The north coast footpath offers mile after mile of majestic cliffs and dramatic rugged scenery. This is easily the most exhilarating walk on the island, and one that can either be done in its entirety over a very long day (roughly eight hours) or in separate sections at a gentler pace. The walk can be done at any time of year, but the scenery is at its best in spring, when sea campion, thrift, ox-eye daisies, pennywort and bluebells are in full bloom. This is also the time of year that you might spot the Glanville fritillary butterfly dancing over the cliffs.

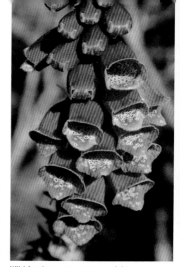

Wild foxgloves are a common sight on the north coast footpath.

Race meetings have been taking place on the island for over one hundred and seventy years. The first races in the 1830s were held on the flat sands of St Aubin's beach, then at Greve d'Azette (St Helier), where several thousand spectators used to

The deserted coast at Plémont.

watch the big events. Gorey Common hosted the races for over sixty years, and special boats used to come from Guernsey for the events. Lillie Langtry, who later bred her own horses, was one of the famous visitors here. Les Landes is a spectacularly located course, but race meetings these days are point-to-point style, without the glamour of bygone days.

Grosnez Castle

At the end of the road, at the most northwesterly point of the island, stand the evocative medieval ruins of the **Castle of Grosnez** ❾. The only recognisable feature is the Gothic arch, although the foundations of walls and buildings beyond it are clearly visible.

A reconstruction on the information panel shows how the castle would have originally looked, complete with drawbridge, portcullis and machicolated upper storey. Unlike Jersey's other main strongholds, little is known of the castle's history.

It was a roughly built fort, constructed in the first half of the fourteenth century in defence against

A lap of honour for a jockey and his horse at Les Landes Race Course, next to the ruins of Grosnez Castle.

an invasion from the French, then destroyed, probably by the French, either in the same century, or when they occupied Jersey in 1461–8. The carved corbels that once decorated the main arch fell off long ago, but

The main gateway, bastions and a narrow moat are all that remain of Grosnez Castle.

were rescued and safely housed in the Archaeological Museum at La Hougue Bie (see page 88). The ruins are set dramatically on the clifftops, 200ft (60 metres) above the rough seas. Walk through the arch for fine views, weather permitting, of all the other Channel Islands.

Looking from left to right these are Guernsey, Jethou, Herm, Sark and in the very far distance, Alderney. The coast of Normandy lies in the distance to the east, while closer inland, a chain of uninhabitable rocks known as **Pater Noster** (Our Father) is visible at low tide.

The name originated from a shipwreck here, involving families who were on their way to colonise the then uninhabited island of Sark. Several of them were drowned, including women and children.

Since then it has been customary for sailors and fishermen to recite the Lord's Prayer as they pass the treacherous reef.

North Coast Footpath

The official **north coast footpath** runs for 15 miles (24km) almost the entire

Walking the north coast footpath is an exhilarating experience.

length of the coast, and offers some of the most dramatically beautiful hiking on the island. Parts of the walk are quite steep, particularly as the path climbs up from the bays, but it can be exhilarating, and there is nothing that

A stone signpost points the way on the north coast footpath.

would really challenge an averagely fit walker. The path occasionally breaks from the coast, diverting through wooded slopes or fields, and in St John's Parish, it joins the main road, following the coast, before heading inland to avoid the unsightly quarry at Ronez.

The public bus service provides the best means of transport – whether you're doing the whole walk or different sections on different days. Services from St Helier operate to points on or close to the north coast (tours 3, 4, 5, 7, 8 and 9), and it's easy to hop off and on.

Bus timetables are available from Visit Jersey, Liberation Bus Station or www.libertybus.je. If you have your own car, leave it at one of the bays and take a bus back to the parking place (although this may involve taking two services, via St Helier).

Although the footpath is well signed and fairly obvious, a map is nevertheless useful. The best one is the Ordnance Survey style Jersey Official Leisure map, available from Visit Jersey or from bookshops.

Take time to admire the flora on your coastal walk.

Eating Out

ROZEL BAY
Château la Chaire Restaurant
Rozel; www.chateau-la-chaire.co.uk.
Behind the bay, in the wooded Rozel valley, this inviting country house hotel offers excellent English cooking with a Gallic influence, in a delightful dining room or in the conservatory with terrace in summer. £££

The Rozel
La Vallée de Rozel;
www.rozelpubanddining.co.uk.
Inn with stone and wood floors, real ales and bar billiards. ££

BOULEY BAY
Mad Mary's
Bouley Bay Beach, Trinity.
Lovely sea-view terrace where you can enjoy crab sandwiches, home-made cakes, bacon butties, cream teas and Mary's legendary hot chocolate with cream and marshmallows. £

BONNE NUIT
Bonne Nuit Beach Café
Bonne Nuit Beach;
www.bonnenuitbeachcafe.co.uk.
One of the north coast's most popular cafés, looking on to the lovely Bonne Nuit Bay and serving everything Thai and other dishes. The café is not licensed so bring your own bottle. £–££

ST JOHN
Les Fontaines
La Route du Nord; https://randalls-jersey.co.uk/les-fontaines-tavern.
Charming country pub on the north coast road close to Sorel Point, converted from a seventeenth century farmhouse with a pleasant sea-view terrace and good pub food. Indoor and outdoor play areas. ££

GRÈVE DE LECQ
Le Moulin de Lecq
Le Mont de la Grève de Lecq;
www.moulindelecq.com.
This traditional, landmark inn was originally a corn mill, parts of which date back to the twelfth century, and is attached to the island's largest working water wheel. Plenty of character (the bar area is built around the old cogwheels), with a varied menu (both traditional dishes as well as several gluten free and vegan options), garden with adventure playground. ££

PLÉMONT
Plémont Beach Café
Tel: 01534-482 005.
This café above Plémont Beach prides itself on supporting local food and art, which is reflected in both the menu and the decor. £

HALL OF FAME

For a tiny island, Jersey can boast some big names, from painters, poets and novelists to golfers and racing drivers, the most celebrated being the actress Lillie Langtry.

The nineteenth century saw political exiles and literati, lured by the coastal scenery and healthy climate, while in more recent times running from the Inland Revenue has been the main reason for celebrities to settle here.

Lillie Langtry 1853–1929

"She has no right to be intelligent, daring and independent as well as lovely." (George Bernard Shaw). The only daughter of a philandering Rector of St Saviour and Dean of Jersey,

Emilie Charlotte Le Breton was born in the parish of St Saviour in 1853. At 21 she married a wealthy widower, Edward Langtry, and two years later took London society by storm with her beauty, vivacity and charm. Among her many famous admirers were Oscar Wilde, who once referred to her as "the second Helen of Troy", President Roosevelt, who noted "She's so pretty she takes away man's breath". But the most famous admirer was the Prince of Wales, later to become Edward VII, a

Lillie Langtry in all her glory.

service for over thirty years, visited Jersey to research the delivery of mail and introduced the pillar box in St Helier in 1854 – the first in the British Isles.

George Eliot (1819–80). The novelist came to Jersey in 1857 with her lover, George Lewes, and was disowned by her family.

John Everett Millais (1829–96), a founder member of the Pre-Raphaelite brotherhood. He became a fashionable painter of portraits and genre pieces. His painting of Lillie Langtry, *A Jersey Lily*, is in the Jersey Museum.

Karl Marx and **Friedrich Engels**, founders of modern socialism, made several visits to Jersey between 1857 and 1885. This was probably for health reasons as they were hardly polite about the island, or its visitors.

Harry Vardon (1870–1937). Professional golfer. Winner of the American Open, the German Open and six times winner of the British Open. He was born in Grouville, Jersey.

Gerald Durrell (1925–95). Celebrated author and naturalist, who set up Jersey Zoo (now the Durrell Wildlife Conservation Trust) in 1959.

Jack Higgins (1929–2022, real name Harry Patterson). Author of over sixty novels, including *The Fox*, set in Jersey during the Occupation, and *The Eagle has Landed*. Lived in Jersey.

Nigel Mansell (b.1953). Former British racing driver who won the Formula One World Championship in 1992. Mansell moved to Jersey in 1997 and has a mansion at St Brelade's Bay. His motoring memorabilia can be viewed at The Mansell Collection (www.themansellcollection.co.uk).

Henry Cavill (b.1983). The film star, perhaps best known for playing Superman/Clark Kent in Man of Steel and Sherlock Holmes in Enola Holmes, was born in St Helier.

womaniser who took "the Jersey Lily" as his mistress. Many years later she caused further furore by becoming the first society woman to take to the stage. Lillie toured the US and South Africa as an actress, became a racehorse owner, and spent her last years in Monaco, where she died at the age of 75. She is buried in the graveyard of St Saviour's Church, next to the rectory where she was born.

Jersey Connections

Sir Walter Raleigh (1552–1618). Governor of Jersey, who named Elizabeth Castle after his revered queen.

Victor Hugo (1802–85). Novelist, poet and dramatist who lived in Jersey from 1852–55 (see page 98).

Anthony Trollope (1815–82). The English novelist worked for the postal

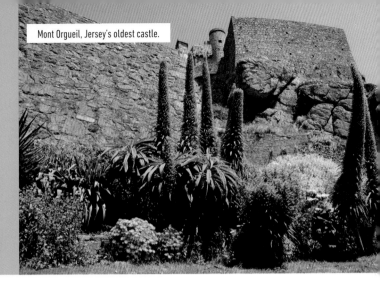

Mont Orgueil, Jersey's oldest castle.

TOUR 6
Sights of the East

History, gastronomy, gardens and beaches – the southeast has it all, and this exciting 18-mile (30km) whole-day driving or cycling tour caters for all tastes.

Mont Orgeuil Castle, set spectacularly above Gorey harbour and commanding the entire east coast, is the most photographed landmark on the island. The medieval fortress played a major role in Jersey's tempestuous history, repulsing repeated French invasions from 1204–1600. The quaint harbour below Mont Orgueil Castle and the spacious sands of the Royal Bay of Grouville provide a pleasant break from sightseeing, while the gardens of Samarès Manor are the highlight of the return trip to town.

A legacy of more ancient history is La Hougue Bie, a finely preserved Neolithic passage grave, its mound a dominant feature of the landscape for 6,000 years.

Highlights

- La Hougue Bie
- Mont Orgueil Castle
- Gorey Harbour
- Royal Bay of Grouville
- Samarès Manor

Take the St Helier ring road, following signs first for the north and then for the A7 to the Five Oaks roundabout. This will take you through the parish of St Saviour, where actress Lillie Langtry (see page 82), was born. She was married twice in the **Church of St Saviour**, and is buried in the churchyard here. Government House, south of the church, is the official residence of the Lieutenant-

Governor, the Queen's representative on the island.

La Hougue Bie

At the Five Oaks roundabout, turn right on to Princes Tower Road (the B28). From here follow the signs for **La Hougue Bie** ❶ (www.jersey heritage.org). This remarkable site, in the heart of the countryside, is dominated by a burial mound, covering a Neolithic passage grave, dating from about 3500 BC. The word "Hougue" derives from the Norse *haugre*, meaning a burial mound, and the "Bie" was probably a corruption of the Norman family name of Hambye. The site can

be a bit confusing, and it's worth watching the short film presentation near the entrance before you start your visit.

This intriguing site abounds with legends, and notably the tales of the dragon which lived in the marshes of St Lawrence and terrified the islanders. Hearing of their plight, the gallant Seigneur of Hambye came from his castle in Normandy and slew the dragon. After the long battle he fell asleep and his squire, who had designs on his master's wife, murdered him and buried the body.

The squire returned to Hambye, leading the wife to believe that the dragon had killed her husband and

La Hougue Bie is one of the largest and best-preserved passage graves in Europe and dates back to 3500 BC.

he (the squire) had gallantly slain the dragon. The Seigneur's dying wish, he told her, was for his wife to marry the servant who had avenged his death. She agreed to marry the squire but the new Lord Hambye soon disclosed his guilt in his sleep. On discovering the truth Lady Hambye came to Jersey and buried her husband under a mound (La Hougue Bie) on the site of his grave. She ordered the mound to be built so high she could spy it from her castle keep in France. The mound was named La Hougue Hambye.

History of La Hougue Bie

Excavations under the mound in 1924 revealed a low passage leading to chambers made of huge stone blocks. The mound is 40ft (12 metres) high and covers a chamber that is 33ft (10 metres) long. The larger stone slabs may have been dragged from a distance of 4 miles (6km), possibly on sledges or rollers. Fragments of bone from eight bodies, along with flint tools, bones of sheep, pig and ox, beads and pottery were all discovered within the dolmen. Limpet shells were also found here, proving that way back in prehistoric times the farmers were enjoying Jersey seafood.

The old pagan site had been Christianised by the construction of two medieval chapels on top of the mound. The first was Notre Dame de la Clarté, dating from the twelfth century, but heavily restored.

Inside the chapel of Notre Dame de la Clarté at La Hougue Bie.

Inside the geology and archaeology museum at La Hougue Bie are fine examples of flint tools found at La Cotte de St Brelade.

Four centuries later the local dean rebuilt its chancel, which became known as the **Jerusalem Chapel**. During the Reformation the chapels were abandoned, but in the late 18th century were transformed by Philippe d'Auvergne, Duke of Bouillon, a scholar and eminent sea captain. Straddling the two chapels he built **The Prince's Tower** (La Tour d'Auvergne as it was known), a neo-Gothic folly which became one

of the most distinctive and dramatic landmarks of the island. In the early nineteenth century the tower became one of Jersey's first tourist attractions, offering panoramic views. In the late 1830s it was extended to create the Prince's Tower Hotel, which became popular for eating, drinking and dancing. But by the late nineteenth century the tower was derelict. A restoration committee in 1924 decided – against the wishes of most of the

Dean Mabon's Miracles

Richard Mabon, Dean of Jersey from 1509, built a small oratory under the Jerusalem Chapel, which was inspired by his pilgrimage to the Holy Sepulchre in Jerusalem. Mabon claimed to receive visions of the Virgin Mary while he was praying in the crypt and organised for pilgrims to visit the site. According to a Protestant chronicler, the Dean used to fake miracles here, making money from gullible pilgrims.

Two chapels under one roof at La Hougue Bie.

islanders – that the Prince's Tower be demolished so that the medieval chapels could be restored to their original form.

Visiting La Hougue Bie

To access the burial chamber below the mound you have to stoop right down and walk along the dark, tunnel-like passage grave. The mysterious chamber, together with the side chambers, is likely to have served not only for burials but as a ritual and ceremonial site (not that there's much space for festivities). From the bottom of the mound a spiral path winds up to the chapels on the top. Switch on the lights in the Jerusalem Chapel to see the traces of two archangels on the wall.

At ground level you can visit the geology and archaeology museum, which displays bones and teeth of prehistoric animals discovered at La Cotte de St Brelade (see page 41). A legacy of more recent history is the German command bunker at the foot of the mound, housing a poignant exhibition dedicated to slave workers

Jersey coat of arm at Mont Orgueil Castle.

in the Channel Islands. The Germans also constructed a watchtower on top of the mound at the west end (no longer extant) and seventy trenches within the grounds.

Mont Orgueil Castle

Turn right out of La Hougue Bie and follow the signs for **Gorey** on the east coast. Nearing the village, a steep road

Built on the site of an Iron Age hill fort, Mont Orgueil Castle stood up to several full-scale attacks between the 13th and 15th centuries.

Taking in the views from the castle battlements.

Somerset Tower

A climb up the steep castle battlements to Somerset Tower will reward you with a jaw-dropping panorama. You can see why the Germans adapted the tower as an observation post in World War II. France can usually be seen across the water, and on a really clear day you can make out the power station at Cap de la Hague on the tip of the Cherbourg peninsula.

brings you down to that most famous of Jersey landmarks, **Mont Orgueil Castle ❷** (www.jerseyheritage.org). Translated as Mount Pride, and also known as Gorey Castle, this mighty fortress towers over the harbour and commands spectacular views. A fine example of a concentric castle, it was sited on an Iron Age hill fort and designed with a series of independent defences, with walls going straight out of the rock.

The castle is an impressive site at any time of day, but it is particularly picturesque after dark in summer when the battlements are floodlit.

Impregnable fortress

From 1204, when King John lost the English territories in France and the Channel Islands elected to remain loyal to the English crown, hostilities prevailed between the islands and France. Jersey was frequently threatened by invasions, and fortifications were constructed, particularly along the vulnerable east coast, lying just 14 miles (22km) from Normandy.

Mont Orgueil was built on a promontory overlooking the French coast and remained the main stronghold on the island for nearly four centuries. The great medieval

fortress withstood many attacks from the French, including a devastating raid in 1373 by the Constable of France, Bertrand du Guesclin, otherwise known as the Black Dog of Brittany. During its long history, the castle fell just once, in 1461, and a French force captured and held the island for the next seven years. Although the castle had been adapted to accommodate cannon, and later

Detail of an equestrian statue in the castle grounds.

Children can raid the dressing-up box at Mont Orgueil Castle, and spend their visit transformed into a medieval queen or a knight in shining armour.

transformed into an artillery fortress, it could not keep up with the demands of modern-day warfare.

In the late sixteenth century the decision was taken to build a new fortress, Elizabeth Castle, in St Aubin's Bay. Mont Orgueil became redundant and known as *Le Vieux Château*. Were it not for the intervention of Sir Walter Raleigh, who thought it a shame to lose such a "stately fort", the castle would have been razed to the ground.

In the 17th and 18th centuries the castle played various roles: a stronghold

of the Royalists in the English Civil War, a state prison under Cromwell, an island prison for those identified as witches, a refuge for French aristocrats and the headquarters of a spy network during the French Revolution. You can still see the chamber where William Prynne, the seventeenth-century puritan, began his sentence. Not only incarcerated, he had his ears cut off and the initials S.L. (Seditious Libeller) branded upon his cheek. In 1907 the castle was given to the people of Jersey by the crown for use as a historic

Birds are trained using techniques dating from the Middle Ages.

Living History

May to October a series of events from Jersey Heritage bring to life the island's history through costumed interpretations, set against the backdrop of historic sites. At Mont Orgueil Castle see medieval swordsmen practising their skills, or perhaps enjoy music and juggling performed by the court jesters, or watch a demonstration of medieval falconry. See www.jerseyheritage.org for a list of what's on.

One of many sculptures inside the castle.

monument and visitor attraction. In 1940 the Germans fortified the site with observation towers, trenches and gun emplacements, and the keep was used as a barracks.

Climbing the ramparts

It's a long haul to the top, via cobbled passages, paths and some two hundred steps, with fine views all the way. En route you can explore towers, batteries, cellars, chapels, medieval halls – and more. A series of stand-alone exhibits are scattered throughout the castle, all providing a flavour of the medieval era and Jersey's role within it. These are mostly sculptures, many of them very striking, ranging from replica Tudor artillery pieces and life-size figures manning the ramparts to witches and warriors, a urine wheel (used by medieval physicians to diagnose patients by the colour of their urine) and the gory *Wound Man*, pierced by spears and daggers. Keeping history alive, there are experts demonstrating Tudor hawking and military weapons, medieval singers, a room of dressing up clothes and wooden soldiers with bows and arrows at the ready.

Gorey Harbour

In the shadow of the castle lies the quaint harbour of **Gorey** ❸, where shops, pubs and cafés cluster around the waterfront. The quayside offers plenty of places to stop for a bite, among them Feast, see page 99.

The original village expanded in the late eighteenth and early nineteenth centuries when the flourishing oyster industry gave Gorey the sobriquet of "the pearl of the east". Oysters were discovered on the muddy seabed between Jersey and Normandy in 1797. The catches were exported to England in large quantities and the trade flourished. Following the decline of the oyster fishing trade at Whitstable, hundreds of English oyster fishermen invaded the coast to share in the profits. By the 1830s the village had doubled in size; there were two hundred and fifty oyster fishing ships, bringing in around 12,000 oysters on each trip. By the middle of the century

A view of the castle gardens and Gorey harbour.

Jersey oysters are cultivated on the rugged east coast near La Rocque.

the oyster beds had been over-fished and the industry was all but over. You can still find a few oysters on the rocks, but those on your plate will have been nurtured in farms in Grouville Bay, where over four million oysters are now produced annually.

Gorey harbour today protects a fleet of pleasure craft and is the only official seaport in Jersey apart from St Helier, however the high-speed

St Helier to Paris

By 1881 you could buy a through ticket all the way from St Helier to Paris. You travelled with the Jersey Eastern Railway Company to Gorey station, by horse and cart to Gorey pier, then a steamer across to Carteret and from here on the new railway line to Paris. However, the company suffered competition from buses, introduced in Jersey in the 1920s, and in 1929 it went into liquidation.

catamaran trips to the port of Carteret in Normandy now run from St Helier.

St Catherine's Bay

From Gorey, follow the coastal B29 north. The road skirts the pebble and sandy bay of Anne Port, and follows the coast by the bay of Havre de Fer and past the distinctive red-and-white **Archirondel Tower**, built in 1874. The tower has recently been restored and can now be hired for basic holiday lets through Jersey Heritage. Keep to the B29 for **St Catherine's Bay ❹**, enclosed to the north by a 0.6-mile (1km) -long breakwater which was built as a result of a British blunder in the mid-nineteenth century.

In answer to a naval base at Cherbourg and other French coastal installations, the British Government chose this site (as well as one at Alderney) for a harbour. Despite warnings that the depth of water was insufficient and the harbour would silt up, the project nevertheless went ahead and a breakwater was

The Archirondel Tower at St Catherine's Bay.

Geoffrey's Leap

North of Gorey the coast road climbs up towards the rocky promontory known as Le Saut Geoffroi or Geoffrey's Leap, named after a convicted criminal and renowned womaniser who managed to survive unscathed after his punishment of jumping from the cliffs to the rocks below. He was declared a freed man but, eager to impress the fair sex, he decided to perform the feat again. This time, however, his luck ran out.

built here, with another one started at Archirondel. Twenty years and £250,000 later, the project was abandoned. The St Catherine's arm of the harbour was preserved and a lighthouse built at the end.

Today the breakwater is a popular spot for fishing and promenading, and the Breakwater Café offers good views from its outdoor tables, see page 99.

Just south of the breakwater is a German bunker, which for several years until recently housed a turbot farm.

The coast road stops at this northern end of St Catherine's Bay, but you can get to Fliquet Bay to the north on foot.

Royal Bay of Grouville

East of Gorey Village, the **Royal Bay of Grouville** ❺ stretches for 3 miles (5km) between Gorey and La Rocque Point. Guarding the bay are a number of towers built as coastal defences in the second half of the eighteenth century. These fortifications were armed and manned, but never actually used to defend the island. Some of them have now been converted to private

Beach fun on the Royal Bay of Grouville.

Moon Walk

For a unique experience take a "moonwalk" on the seabed to Seymour Tower. Through guided walks organised by Jersey Walk Adventures (www.jerseywalk adventures.co.uk) you can explore the savage low-tide seascape of gutters, reefs, tidal flats, lagoons, sandbanks and boulder fields – said to resemble the surface of the moon. During night walks the tiny creatures in the water and the seaweed glow in the dark like fireflies or glow worms. Prepare to get your feet wet!

Enjoy a hike across the lunar seascape.

residences. Queen Victoria, so impressed by this long and spacious sandy bay, gave it the Royal prefix after her visit in 1859. Today the beach is popular with sunbathers and water sports enthusiasts. As you go south you'll see the links of the **Royal Jersey Golf Club**, the most exclusive

on the island. Harry Vardon, six times British Open Championship winner, was born in Grouville.

Seymour Tower

The route returns to St Helier via the coast road, the A4, stopping at the little harbour of **La Rocque ❻** on the

The isolated Seymour Tower was built as part of Jersey's coastal defence and dates back to the 18th century.

A statue of Harry Vardon, six times Open golf champion, takes a swing at the Royal Jersey Golf Club.

southeastern tip of the island. It was here that Baron de Rullecourt and his troops secretly landed in January 1781, en route to their defeat at Royal Square in St Helier (see page 20). Low tide reveals a vast lunar landscape of reefs, gullies and rock pools. Seymour Tower, standing on a rocky islet 2 miles (3km) to the southeast,

Green Island is only an island at high tide.

has stood guard over the island since 1782. It can be reached on foot, but beware of the large tidal flow and the rapid incoming waters: the sea can rise 18ins (50cm) in 10 minutes. (Check the times of the tides in the *Jersey Post* or at https://www.gov.je/weather/tidetimes). For the adventurous there is the opportunity of staying at the tower overnight (it sleeps 7). Access is restricted to specific days, dependent on the tides, and all groups must be accompanied by an accredited guide (for further information visit www.jerseyheritage.org).

Green Island

From La Rocque continue on the A4, detouring briefly after 2.5 miles (4km) at **Green Island** ❼, a few hundred metres off the coast and the most southerly in the British Isles. A small rocky outcrop covered in grass (hence the name), it is only an island when the tide is high and is otherwise accessible by foot. Prehistoric graves, along with human and animal bones, were discovered here in 1911, but were removed for safekeeping to the Jersey Museum in St Helier. The island has gradually been eroded by the sea, and

Samarès Manor is an elegant house set in extensive grounds incorporating ornamental gardens and ponds with swans.

restorers are currently trying to prevent it from being washed away.

The main attraction here is the **Green Island Restaurant**, perched at the top of the slope and offering amazing views from the terrace, which is the perfect suntrap in summer (see page 99).

The Herb Garden at Samarès has a unique collection of culinary and medicinal plants.

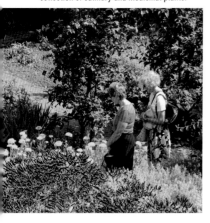

Ramsar Site

This southeastern corner of Jersey, equating to 25 percent of the island's landmass, is designated as a Ramsar Site (Wetland of International Importance), one of four on Jersey. The low-lying south and southeast coast are also prime areas for ornithologists. The vast expanse of mud, sand and rocky outcrops provides a rich breeding ground for thousands of wintering waders, gulls and wildfowl. Plovers, redshank, turnstone, dunlin, bar-tailed godwits, curlew and oystercatchers can be seen on an incoming tide along the rocky shore.

Botanic Gardens at Samarès Manor

Before returning to St Helier, it is well worth making a mile (1.6km) detour north to **Samarès Manor** ❽ (www.samaresmanor.com), with its beautiful and extensive gardens. From Green Island take the narrow Rue de Samarès going north, and

The tranquil water garden has a soothing effect on the visitor.

turn left when you reach the main A5. You'll soon see signs to the manor, off to the right. The name "Samarès" derives from the Old Norman French *Salse Marais*, or saltwater marsh, dating from ancient times when the owners profited from the saltpans on the low-lying land to the south.

The original grounds were designed by Sir James Knott, Tyneside ship owner and philanthropist, who spent the last ten years of his life in Jersey. His enthusiasm for Eastern-style planting is reflected in the exotic Japanese-style rock and water gardens. But Samarès has seen a major program of restoration and diversification over the years, and now there are over 14 acres (6 hectares) of gardens to explore. Guided tours of the gardens are available, and there's a children's play area.

A highlight is the **Herb Garden**, designed by John Brookes and filled with fragrant, medicinal and culinary plants. The Herb Café is a lovely spot to take a break, sited amid the culinary herbs which are used to flavour the dishes. Parts of the manor house, where the owners live, can be visited on guided tours, and there's also the Museum of Agricultural and Rural Life to be visited.

Le Dicq and Victor Hugo

Turn right out of Samarès on to the A5 and you will soon be back on the A4 and the outskirts of St Helier. Just

A Marine Wilderness

The Jersey Ramsar Site, stretching from St Helier Harbour to Gorey Pier, is a marine wilderness, characterised by weather-worn reefs, mud, sand and shingle shores, and exposed twice daily by one of the largest tidal ranges in the world.

The Gulf Stream-warmed waters are home to a rich and valuable ecology. Some 107 species of fish, 57 of crustacea, 113 of mollusc and 230 of seaweed have been recorded – far more than the criteria set by Ramsar.

The gulf stream provides a perfect nutrient-rich breeding ground for oysters.

Victor Hugo gathers inspiration at Le Dicq.

beyond where the two roads merge, on the seaward side, Le Dicq slipway has a plaque to **Victor Hugo**, who lived nearby.

In 1851, when Louis Napoleon staged a coup in France, the French writer and staunch Republican feared for his life and fled from France. He chose Jersey, which had a history of granting asylum to refugees – the Prince of Wales (later Charles II), Huguenots and Royalist revolutionaries among them.

A plaque in honour of Victor Hugo, at La Pomme d'Or Hotel, St Helier.

Hugo stayed at La Pomme d'Or Hotel in St Helier until he was able to find a house by the sea. He lived with his wife and children at 3 Marina Terrace, Greve d'Azette, while his mistress, Juliette Drouais, was conveniently lodged just down the road at Le Havre des Pas.

Hugo's house, which was knocked down in the 1970s, was fairly spartan, but he was close to Le Dicq where he drew inspiration from the sea. He gathered here with other exiles by a large rock, accessible at low tide, known as Le Rocher des Proscrits. In 1855 the exiles' Jersey newspaper, *L'Homme*, published a letter discrediting Queen Victoria for making a state visit to Louis Napoleon – by this time Napoleon III. Jersey was (and still is) supportive of the monarchy and the editor and owner of the newspaper were expelled from the island without trial.

Hugo signed a declaration against the expulsion and as a result was forced to set sail for Guernsey, where he lived for the next fifteen years.

Eating Out

LE DICQ

Longueville Manor

Longueville Road;
www.longuevillemanor.com.
Exclusive country hotel offering
a haven of indulgence. Come for
gourmet cuisine, with local seasonal
produce from the kitchen garden, and
exceptional service and hospitality.
£££

Thai Dicq Shack

Dicq Slipway, Dicq Road, St
Saviour; tel: 01534-730 273;
www.facebook.com/thaidicqshack.
Dig your toes in the sand and tuck
into fresh and fabulous Thai food,
at the island's original Thai eatery.
Bring your own drinks. Takeaway
available most of the year. £–££

ST CATHERINE'S BAY

Breakwater Café

La Route de St Catherine;
https://thebreakwatercafe.com.
Popular spot after a bracing walk
along the pier to sit and watch
the boats go by. It's homely and
unpretentious, with a classic café
menu, all-day breakfasts and popular
ice-cream parlour. £

GROUVILLE

Bass and Lobster Foodhouse

Gorey Coast Road, St Martin;
www.bassandlobster.com.
Michelin-listed restaurant with
a history of championing Jersey
produce, whether it's hand-dived
scallops served with locally grown
butternut squash and truffle purée,
or pan-roasted Jersey sea bass with
softshell crab tempura. Despite the
name there are always non-seafood
dishes available, from venison saddle
to mushroom linguini. £££

Feast

Gorey Pier; www.feast.je.
An island favourite, specialising
in simple freshly cooked cuisine,
from the signature sticky ribs to
imaginative salads and delicious
seafood, with some vegetarian
options. It overlooks the harbour
and magnificent Mont Orgueil Castle.
££–£££

The Moorings

Gorey Pier;
www.themooringshotel.com.
Modern, Michelin-listed restaurant
which is part of the hotel of the
same name. Expect a strong Gallic
influence and plenty of seafood, from
Chancre crab to Malaysian coconut
fruits de mer, along with the likes of
wild pheasant schnitzel, Norwegian
beef and pork meatballs, and some
vegetarian and vegan options, plus
some mouthwatering desserts. £££

Sumas

Gorey Hill;
www.sumasrestaurant.com.
Fresh, innovative cuisine in a stylish
little restaurant overlooking Gorey
harbour and castle – reserve a
table alfresco – with a twist of
Mediterranean flair and legendary
weekend brunch. Book in advance,
especially if you want a terrace table
with outstanding views of Grouville
Bay and Gorey Castle. £££

GREEN ISLAND

Green Island Restaurant and Beach Hut

Green Island; www.greenisland.je.
Soak up the sea views and enjoy
sensational seafood at this waterfront
restaurant, which has a terrace and
elegant indoor dining room. The
menu also features grilled meat
dishes and a (rather more limited)
handful of vegetarian options. Despite
a location that feels exclusive, it's
easy to get to, with ample free
parking. ££–£££

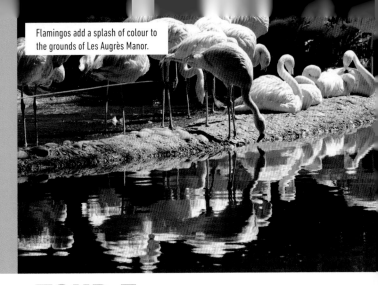

Flamingos add a splash of colour to the grounds of Les Augrès Manor.

TOUR 7
Durrell's Wildlife

"You can't build a tortoise. You can't build a bird. That's what we've got to remember – if we destroy it, we can't recreate it." Gerald Durrell (1925–95).

From the age of six, when he lived in central India, Gerald Durrell kept a collection of animals and dreamt of having his own zoo. His first collection included "everything from minnows to woodlice"; then, when his family moved to Corfu during the 1930s, his menagerie extended to "everything from eagle owls to scorpions". His animal adventures on the Greek island – along with the antics of his family – are humorously described in his best-selling book *My Family and Other Animals* (1956). The hit TV series The Durrells (2016-18) was based on Durrell's three autobiographical books about his years living on tCorfu.

At 21 Durrell inherited £3,000 and used it to fund an animal-collecting expedition to the British Cameroons. In 1957, after several other major expeditions to far-flung parts of the world to collect

This way for flamingos and gorillas, that way for bats and lemurs.

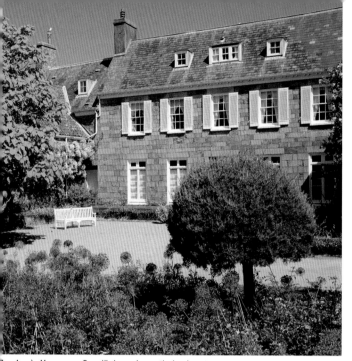

Les Augrès Manor, once Durrell's home, is now the headquarters of the Durrell Wildlife Conservation Trust.

animals on behalf of zoos, the pioneering naturalist and author founded what was then known as the Jersey Wildlife Preservation Trust. The name was later changed to the Durrell Wildlife Conservation Trust, then to the Durrell Wildlife Park – or simply Durrell – and now it is called Jersey Zoo. For many years this has been the island's prime visitor attraction. This is no ordinary zoo with the usual elephants and giraffes. It is entirely devoted to the preservation of animal life and has become internationally renowned as a sanctuary and breeding centre for some of the world's most endangered species.

Durrell's Legacy

For over sixty years the Trust has been working on saving species from extinction, building up colonies and reintroducing them to their original homes. As the symbol of the Trust Durrell chose the dodo, demonstrating his commitment to saving rare species from the fate of the flightless bird from Mauritius.

Durrell Souvenirs

The Durrell shop has an excellent range of animal-related products, such as Gerald Durrell's books (he wrote no less than 37) including *My Family and Other Animals* (his amusing animal adventures on Corfu), zoo videos, limited edition ceramics, gorilla posters, soft toy orang-utans, Livingstone fruit bats and lemurs, jigsaws and souvenirs with the Durrell (dodo) symbol.

Feeding time is a popular time, not just for the animals, but the visitors too.

In the early days Durrell's efforts at captive breeding were dismissed by many eminent zoologists. He was one of the first to draw attention to what was happening in the environment, and fifty years on virtually every reputable zoo follows at least some of the principles that he put into practice here in Jersey.

The perfect setting

Since the zoo opened in 1959 over 13,000 animals have been born here, and several species have been saved from extinction and reintroduced into their original habitats. Gerald Durrell died in 1995, and at his memorial service David Attenborough spoke of the zoo's priorities: "the animals first, the staff

Visitor Information

Getting There: Jersey Zoo, Les Augrès Manor, La Profonde Rue, Trinity (4 miles/6km north of St Helier), accessed on the B31; www.durrell.org. Bus routes: 3, 13 and 23.
Some amazing animal experiences and guided tours are offered, giving you the opportunity to see and learn about a species up-close – including meerkats, fruit bats and lemurs – from a keeper-only area or even within the enclosure itself. These special experiences must be pre-booked well in advance – group sizes are small, usually a maximum of just four visitors, so you need to apply for a place on these 4–6 weeks ahead of your visit.

Durrell's famous memoirs.

White-handed gibbons move around by swinging their body along using alternate handholds.

second and the public as privileged paying guests". Durrell's zoologist wife, Lee, is executor of the Durrell estate and continues the work of the Trust.

The setting is a 32-acre (13 hectare) oasis of woodland, landscaped lawns and water gardens, surrounding an eighteenth-century granite manor house. There are over 130 species of animals, birds and reptiles, and the Durrell International Training Centre which has seen over three thousand students from 128 countries since it opened in 1984. The ex-students are now in charge of some of the most important conservation projects in the world.

Wherever possible, the trust has tried to cultivate the native habitat of the animals' wildlife. Compared to most zoos, the enclosures are spacious and imaginative, and the animals do look remarkably content. The **golden-headed lion tamarins** roam in the woodlands, the **gorillas** lounge in their spacious compound, the **aye-ayes** have a special nocturnal unit and the **rope-haired orang-utans** swing happily from their ropes.

Saved from the Brink

The Trust mainly focuses on the island areas of the Galápagos, Caribbean islands, Madagascar, Indian Ocean islands and India. Among the success stories are species which,

Loggers in the Amazon Basin are becoming a threat to the highly intelligent, silvery marmoset.

A Sumatran orang-utan collects his take-away lunch.

Minister of St Lucia who travelled to Jersey especially to escort them home.

Among other projects are the **Floreana mockingbird** from the Galápagos and the **Montserrat mountain chicken**, a large frog that is in danger of extinction from a fungal disease. Closer to home, Durrell works with local wildlife groups to help save the declining population of Jersey's green lizard and the symbolic Jersey *crapaud* or common toad.

A moated enclosure near the entrance is home to a family of ring-tailed coatis, howler monkeys and a pair of **Andean bears**, Quechua and Bahia. The only bears in South America, the species is being pushed to extinction by the destruction of their natural habitats and the huge demand for bear blood, bile and organs used in traditional medicine and delicacies such as bear paw soup.

Gentle Jambo

Favourite inmates of the zoo are the **Sumatran orang-utans**, who provide endless entertainment in their splendid

through captive breeding, have been reintroduced to Mauritius.

These include the Mauritius kestrels, the **echo parakeet** and the **pink pigeons** – distant relations of the dodo. The Trust is currently concentrating on restoring the ecosystems of the small islands of Mauritius that were once rich habitats of wildlife. Other species which have been brought back from the brink are the **golden lion tamarins** which have been released in a private reserve in Brazil, the **thick-billed parrots**, considered extinct in Arizona, which are now flying free in their native pinewoods, the **St Lucia whiptail lizard**, the **Mallorcan midwife toad** and the **Assam pygmy hog**, the smallest pig in the world.

In 1989 a pair of **St Lucia Amazon parrots**, the national bird, flew courtesy of British Airways back to the Caribbean, accompanied by the Prime

Adopt an Animal

It was Durrell's dream to close down the Trust because it would no longer be necessary, as there weren't any endangered species. But he knew it wouldn't happen. "The world is being destroyed at the speed of an Exocet missile, and we are riding a bicycle," he said of his work. "I feel despair 24 hours a day." The Trust was – and still is – plagued by financial problems and as a charity depends on public help. You can give support by adopting an animal, becoming a member, booking an animal encounter, donating to Durrell or buying a souvenir (further information at www.durrell.org).

Animal Experiences

At Jersey Zoo you can do more than just see the animals. There are options to roll up your sleeves and be a keeper for the day, help to feed the animals, muck in and make them feel at home. Or choose from 'Animal Experiences', meeting the meerkats, apes or reptiles. See www.durrell.org for more information and costs.

habitat of islands and waterways; the **Livingstone fruit bats**, with a wingspan of 6ft (almost 2 metres); and – most famous of all – the **western lowland gorillas**.

Beside the compound a statue commemorates Jambo, the mighty silver-back gorilla who shot to international stardom in 1986 when he stood over a five-year-old boy who fell into the enclosure, protecting him from the rest of the gorillas. The "gentle giant", who fathered thirteen offspring and died in 1992,

Bronze statue of Jambo, the "gentle giant".

was the first male gorilla to be reared in captivity.

For a unique experience animal lovers can camp out in luxury at the Durrell Wildlife Camp (see page 125), with unlimited access to the park.

Oriental short-clawed otters live in the redeveloped valley.

Cycle routes in Jersey

Route
1

St. Catherine 1¾ ↑

Gorey Village 2½ →

END OF ROUTE 1

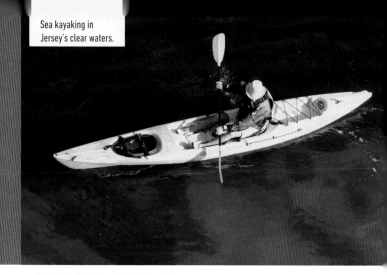

Sea kayaking in Jersey's clear waters.

TRIP TIPS
Active Pursuits

From surfing and skydiving to fishing and golf, Jersey has a host of activities to keep you occupied.

Sports enthusiasts are spoilt for choice on Jersey, whether it's on the water or ashore. In an effort to rejuvenate its image, the island has introduced a range of adventure sports in recent years. Along with the usual, long-established activities such as surfing and sailing, you can try out sports such as skydiving, blokarting, kiteboarding, abseiling and stand-up paddle-boarding. The Visit Jersey website (www.jersey.com) is packed with information on all the activities on the island and the companies which operate them.

Walking

Jersey has a walk for every day of the year, from dramatic rugged cliffs to the leafy lanes of the interior. The island may be small, but it offers some surprisingly dramatic and varied scenery, particularly along the northern coastline. Here the footpath follows the coast for most of the way, dipping down to fishing villages where you can take a break at beachside cafés.

Jersey Tourism publishes a free pamphlet with ideas for walks, from north coast walking routes to reservoir walks and 'Ice Age' trails, with a map provided. Specialist guided walks are numerous, with themes ranging from Victorian Jersey and World War II to the Oyster Trail and hidden gardens. One of the most fascinating is the "moonwalk", taking you across the lunar-like seascape at the south-eastern tip of the island. This gigantic rock pool disappears below the sea twice a day. Information on guided walks can be found at www.jersey.com and for self-guided walks see https://www.nationaltrust.je/walks.

For self-guided walks, forget the car and get around the island with the

The Railway Walk

The now defunct Western Railway track, linking St Helier with St Aubin and later extended to La Corbière, has been turned into a foot and cycle path. This makes an enjoyable, unchallenging, tree-lined walk (or cycle ride) ending up at La Corbière, where you can walk out to the lighthouse providing the tide is not too high. If you do not want to make the return journey on foot, buses will take you back to St Aubin or St Helier.

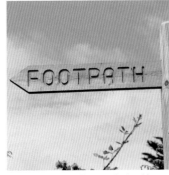

Some of the finest walks are to be found in Jersey, both along the coast and inland.

help of the excellent bus service. Time tables are available from the tourist office or bus station in St Helier, or at www.libertybus.je. The best map is the Ordnance Survey Jersey Official Leisure Map. When exploring the coast, visitors should watch out for extreme tidal movement, one of the largest recorded in the world.

Inland walks

The rural interior offers walks through woodlands, valleys and reservoirs. The path alongside Waterworks Valley, running north from Millbrook, follows the winding road past reservoirs and through wooded slopes. To the west, the Jersey War Tunnels (www. jerseywartunnels.com) is a good starting point for walks through attractive woodland along St Peter's Valley. In the northeast of the island, there are delightful walks in the thickly wooded valley of Rozel Woods, between St Catherine's Bay and St Martin's Village. The path circling the Y-shaped Val de la Mare reservoir is an easy 3-mile (5km) walk, providing fine views of the distant St Ouen's Bay from near the dam. Queen's Valley Reservoir, west of Gorey, provides another pleasant, undemanding walk which takes you around the trout-filled waters.

In June keen hikers flock to Jersey for the sponsored 48-mile (77km) Island Walk around the island. Expect to complete the course in anything between 12–21 hours. Funds go to Jersey charities – over the 31 years it has been taking place, the annual event has raised over £2.7 million in sponsorship.

Cycling

No distance on Jersey is too far to cycle, and the network of quiet country lanes and coastal

Walking in Rozel Woods.

roads makes for pleasant, if at times strenuous, cycling. A 96-mile (155km) network has been established all over the island, and the clear signs along the way enable you to explore the winding lanes without constantly referring to maps. The routes take in the Green Lanes, where pedestrians, cyclists and horse-riders have priority over cars, and motorists must slow down to a sedate 15mph (24kmh). If a rural lane suddenly ceases to be a Green Lane, the probability is you have cycled across a parish boundary; two parishes (Trinity and St Saviour) are still resisting the Green Lane scheme.

Visitors who want to plan their own cycling itineraries should consult the Visit Jersey website (www.jersey.com) for detailed cycling routes. The Island Tourist Map includes cycle routes marking the coastal circuit, inland links and connections to various popular attractions.

For cycle hire, see Practical Information (see page 118).

Surfing

St Ouen's Bay, with its huge rollers and spacious sands, is a paradise for surfers. The first surf club to open here was the Jersey Surfboard Club (www.jerseysurfboardclub.com) – established in 1959 and one of the first in Europe. This and other clubs hire out surf equipment and offer tuition. You can also learn to kitesurf, propelling yourself at high speeds across the sea on a surfboard with a large controllable kite. The oldest surfing school on the island is Jersey Surf School (https://jerseysurfschool. co.uk), in La Braye.

Bodyboarding is hugely popular along the bay, from the old guard who still use wooden boards to youngsters in wetsuits with the latest gear. Equipment can be hired at any of the surf schools. The seas are rough, with rip tides and strong currents. Inexperienced surfers should always keep to the areas between flags, which are patrolled by lifeguards. Red flags indicate the conditions are dangerous.

Kitesurfing at St Ouen's Bay.

Casting off on the rocks at St Catherine's Bay.

Experienced windsurfers enjoy skimming along the sea at St Ouen's, but the more sheltered bays of St Brelade's Bay, St Aubin's or Grouville are a lot more suitable for learners. The water sports centres on these bays also offer paddle -boarding, waterskiing, wakeboarding, banana rides, rowing boats and canoes.

Sailing and boat tours

Marinas and harbours have excellent facilities for sailors but beginners should beware of sunken reefs, big tides and strong currents. Experienced sailors can charter boats or join local regattas. For yacht charter, private skippered charter trips, catamaran island tours or learning to sail contact Go Sail (www.go-sail.je). Jersey Seafaris (www.jerseyseafaris.com) run rib boat tours out to Les Minquiers, which include the southernmost sandbank in the British Isles, as well as elsewhere.

Sea Kayaking/Coasteering

Jersey's clear waters, remote coves and rich marine life make for excellent kayaking and coasteering. The kayak specialists are Jersey Kayak Adventures (www.jerseykayakadventures.co.uk) who operate from beaches all over the island. Absolute Adventures (www.absoluteadventures.je) on St Brelade's Bay organize coasteering, sea kayaking, blokarting (for which the broad sands at St Ouen's Bay make a perfect location), wakeboarding and other adventure sports.

Fishing/rockpooling

Sea bass, wrasse, grey mullet, bream, pollack and mackerel and occasionally conger eel are caught offshore. For deep-sea fishing trips, by day or night,

Cider barrels at Hamptonne Country Life Museum.

Leisure and Fitness

Keep in trim at Fitness First at the Waterfront Centre (www.fitness firstjersey.com) in St Helier, equipped with gym, sauna and steam room. The next door Aqua Splash (www.aquasplash.je) has a 25-metre, six-lane swimming pool, and outdoor pool with flumes, slides and diving area.

Aqua Splash has indoor and outdoor pools.

contact David Nuth, tel: 01534-858 046 or 07797-728 316 (www.tarkasea trips.com). The piers on the north coast are popular for rod fishing.

For young children there are numerous rock pools where you can catch crabs, shrimps and devil fish. Every beach shop sells cheap nets and buckets. At St Aubin's Bay during spring tides you can sprinkle salt on the keyhole-shaped burrow of razor fish and watch them pop up out of their holes.

Diving

The sea in Jersey is clean, visibility is good and marine life plentiful. Most of the diving takes place at Bouley Bay on the north coast, where the waters are particularly clear and conditions normally calm. The Bouley Bay Diving School (https://scubadivingjersey. com) is a PADI 5-star diving centre which welcomes divers of all standards, including beginners. More experienced divers can visit the wrecks of ships sunk in World War II and other vessels which have been scuttled to provide shelter for marine life.

Beaches and Swimming

The water temperatures are on the cool side (averaging around 17°C/63°F in summer), which does have the

A hole-in-one at the Royal Jersey Golf Club.

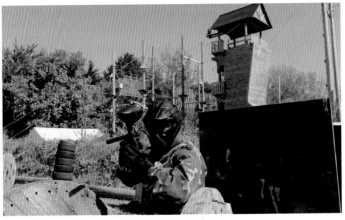

Playing soldiers on the assault course at Valley Adventure Centre.

advantage that the seas are crowd-free. The beaches are clean, with clear waters, but beware of currents and tides. The main beaches are surveyed by lifeguards during the season. The best beaches for youngsters are St Brelade's, St Aubin and Grouville, where the sand shelves gently and the waters are normally calm. Beauport, west of St Brelade's, accessed down a steep path, is one of the least crowded bays.

Golf

The island has six golf courses. Top of the list is the Royal Jersey Golf Club (www.royaljersey.com) beside Royal Grouville Bay. The club was founded in 1878 and was the training ground of

Grouville-born Harry Vardon, six times winner of the British Open. You need proof of handicap to play here, as you do for La Moye Golf Club at St Brelade (www.lamoyegolfclub.co.uk), which has some stunning views of St Ouen's Bay. Non-club members can play at the 18-hole Les Mielles Golf and Country Club (www.lesmielles.com), the 9-hole courses at Wheatlands, St Peter (www.wheatlandsjersey.com) or Les Ormes, St Brelade (www.lesormes jersey.co.uk).

Blokarting at St Ouen's Bay.

Valley Adventure Centre

This exhilarating activity centre (https://valleyadventure.je) is set in a natural green valley, and provides a host of adventurous pursuits for children and adults. You can try out aerial trekking, tower climbing and abseiling, zip wire, archery and axe-throwing – to name just a few.

Themed Holidays

Themes on Jersey range from German Occupation War trails to yoga retreats by the beach.

Heritage Holidays

Jersey War Tours (www.jerseybunker tours.com) offer evening tours of the island's WW2 bunkers, including sites not otherwise open to the public.

Walking Tours

With **Macs Adventure** (www.macs adventure.com), you can go round the entire island on foot in a week (April to October). B&B accommodation and door-to-door luggage transfers are included. They also offer a 'Channel Islands in Comfort' tour, which combines walking and cultural sites, while island-hopping between Jersey, Guernsey and Sark.

Spa and Gastronomy

The Club Hotel & Spa (www.theclub jersey.com), St Helier's luxury boutique hotel, offers spa packages combining a morning at the Club Spa's thermal suite, a swim in the indoor saltwater poor

Outdoor pool at The Club Hotel & Spa.

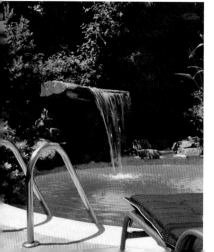

(or private outdoor pool), a massage or facial, and a three-course lunch at the hotel's gourmet Bohemia restaurant.

Surfing

Young surfers can join non-residential summer camps with **Jersey Quicksilver Surf School** (www.jerseysurfschool. co.uk). Five-day activity courses for kids aged 7 and above (participants are required to be able to swim a minimum of 50m unassisted), including at least 2 hours of surfing instruction per day along with other activities.

Bush Camps, outdoor adventure and foraging

Discover wild edible plants, cook on a beach fire and learn natural navigating skills, on overnight or 6-day survival courses, with Kazz at **Wild Adventures** (https://wildadventures jersey.com). The Valley Adventure Centre (www.valleyadventure.je) runs all-year activity clubs for 7-14 year-olds, which include aerial trekking, zip wires, and spring and summer water sports. **Jersey Kayak Adventures** (https://jerseykayakadventures.co.uk) offer tours and kayaking courses.

Conservation

Give something back to the environment with practical conservation work, via the National Trust's volunteer scheme (www.nationaltrust.je). You can also join a volunteering program at Jersey Zoo (www.durrell.org).

Arts

Follow the **St Helier Art Trail** which brings together some of the island's best street art. **Jersey Arts Centre** (www.artscentre.je) runs non-residential art courses and workshops for both children and adults.

Practical Information

Getting There

Year-round air and sea packages, short breaks, flights and accommodation can all be arranged through specialist tour operators such as Jersey Travel (www.jerseytravel. com) and Channel Islands Direct (www.channelislandsdirect.co.uk).

Condor Ferries can arrange sea packages and short breaks (www.condorferries.co.uk). If you have booked accommodation independently, your hotel can normally arrange transport for you, as well as car rental if required. Visit Jersey (www.jersey.com) has detailed information of air and sea travel, plus a list of specialist tour operators.

By air

During the summer direct flights to Jersey operate from around 40 UK airports. From London airports alone there are up to 12 flights a day. Off season the number of flights is reduced, especially from regional airports. The main airlines are easyJet (www.easyjet. com), which flies from Gatwick, Luton, Liverpool, Manchester, , Belfast, Edinburgh and Glasgow, and British Airways (www.ba.com), which operate regular flights from London Heathrow. Blue Islands (www.blueislands.com) flies from Jersey to Southampton, Birmingham, Bristol, Exeter, East Midlands and Norwich.

Many tour operators also offer seasonal charter flights from UK regional airports. For further information click on "Getting Here" on the Visit Jersey website (www.jersey.com). The best prices are normally secured by booking well in advance on the internet and avoiding weekends and the busiest times of year. Both Blue Islands

and Aurigny (www.aurigny.com) provide a Channel Island hopping service between Jersey and Guernsey; Aurigny also includes Alderney.

Jersey airport (www.jerseyairport. com) is 5 miles (8km) west of St Helier in St Peter. Car hire and taxis are available, and three bus routes conect the airport with St Helier – No. 15 via St Aubin (this is a double decker with luggage racks, journey time 30 minutes), No. 22 (an expres service, journey time 20 minutes) and No. 9 via the Rugby Club. Timetables at https://libertybus.je.

By sea

The only ferry line from the UK to Jersey is Condor Ferries (www.condor ferries.co.uk), which operates a high-speed ferry service from Poole. The crossing normally goes via Guernsey and takes 4 hours. It is not uncommon for boats to be cancelled or delayed because of the weather conditions, particularly off season. The state-of-the-art trimaran, Condor *Voyager* accommodates 850

The Commodore Clipper.

passengers and 235 cars, and has on board a cafeteria, bars, soft play area for children and a duty-free shop with some excellent deals. Club-class seating and steward service is available for an extra charge.

Condor Ferries also operates a slower service from Portsmouth on the conventional Commodore car/passenger ferry. The crossing takes 8–11 hours, depending on whether the ferry stops at Guernsey. The return crossing is overnight with the option of 1-, 2-, 3- or 4-berth cabins and en suite facilities.

Fast ferry services from Jersey to Guernsey and St Malo in France are also operated by Condor Ferries.

Visitors bringing their own car must have the vehicle registration document and a valid driving licence or International Driving Permit (photocopies not accepted). Bikes can be taken across free of charge.

Getting Around

Buses

Jersey has an efficient, easy-to-use network of buses, operated by Liberty Bus (www.libertybus.je). All buses radiate from Liberation Station, St Helier. Bus timetables, with a map of the routes and a Liberation Station layout plan, are available from either the bus station, or the nearby tourist office. The website has a journey planner and gives live times. Download the LibertyBus app, which has a TrackMyBus function showing live journeys across the island. Tickets can be bought on board (cash or contactless). A Discover Jersey ticket allows unlimited travel for 1, 2, 3 or 7 days and is available from Liberty Station as well as on board. You can also get a family version (valid for 2 adults and up to 3 children under the age of 15).

The choice is yours.

The amphibious Castle Ferry at Elizabeth Castle, St Helier.

Half-day, evening and whole-day island coach tours are available with a pick-up service from many hotels. Visit Tantivy Blue Coach Tours (www.tantivybluecoach.com) or Waverley Coaches (www.waverleycoaches.co.uk).

Car hire

To hire a car you need to be at least 20 and have held a valid driving licence for at least 12 months, with no endorsements for dangerous or drunken driving in the last five years. UK drivers need to carry a UK license, not an international license. Most companies impose an upper age limit. Rental prices in Jersey are similar to those in the UK and petrol prices slightly cheaper. Car hire companies are abundant and competitive.

Hire firms include: Avis (www.avisjersey.co.uk), Europcar (www.europcarjersey.com) and Hertz, Jersey Airport (www.hertz.co.uk). More companies are listed on the Visit Jersey website www.jersey.com/plan-your-break/getting-around-jersey/car-hire.

Driving

The island's maximum speed limit is 40mph (64kmh), reduced to 30mph or 20mph (48 or 32kmh) in some town areas and to 15mph (24kmh) on Green Lanes, where priority is given

Cycling is an environmentally friendly way of exploring the island.

Green Flag

Jersey was the first holiday destination in the world to be awarded Green Globe Status in recognition of schemes such as the Green Lane network, coastal footpaths and cycle tracks. On the other hand Jersey has one of the highest ratios of cars to people in the world, and this, coupled with the high population density, puts pressure on the environment and infrastructure. The best bet for going green is to travel to Jersey by ferry, cycle around the island or use the excellent network of buses.

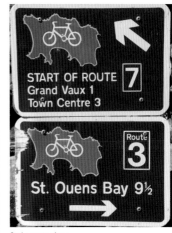

Cycle-route signs.

to pedestrians and cyclists. Part time 20mph (32kmh) limits are in place around schools. Rules of the road are the same as those of the UK: driving is on the left, seat belts are compulsory, and it is an offence to hold a mobile phone whilst driving. Fixed alcohol limits and roadside breath testing are similar to the UK. Penalties are severe, with up to £2,000 fine or 6 months' imprisonment for the first offence plus unlimited disqualification of your driving licence.

Parking requires the use of either a yellow disco or Paycard, available from Visit Jersey, Condor Ferries, hire-car companies, post offices, shops or anywhere displaying the Paycard logo (a blue P inside a red C). The cards are available as individual units or in books of ten. The PayByPhone app shows all paid parking on the island, and can be used to pay for parking.

Cycling

See Active Pursuits, page 108. Bikes can be hired from Jersey Bike Hire, (www.jerseybikehire.co.uk). If you are travelling with Condor Ferries, bikes can be brought over from the UK free of charge.

Inter-island ferries and France

Condor (see also "By Sea") operate a high-speed car ferry service between St Malo and Jersey (2hrs 20 minutes).

There is a good supply of cycle shops and hire facilities in Jersey.

From April to September Manche-iles-express (www.manche-iles.com/en) operate passenger services from St Helier to Sark and Guernsey, as well as to Granville and Carteret in Normandy, and from Guernsey to Diélette. Passports are required for France. There are places for six bicycles on board.

Condor Ferries operate day trips to Guernsey, with ferry connections on to Sark and Herm.

Taxis

Taxis on Jersey are expensive. Ranks are located at the airport, harbour and St Helier. Otherwise call Domino Cabs: 01534-747 047; Liberty Cabs: 01534-767 700; or Yellow Cabs: 01534-888 888.

Facts for the Visitor

Accessible travel

For detailed information covering accommodation, transport, parking, attractions and equipment available to hire for travellers with disabilities, visit www.jersey.com/accessible-jersey. Maison des Landes is a hotel designed specifically for disabled guests. On-street parking and public car parks have designated areas for UK and European Blue Badge holders. Public conveniences fitted with radar locks can be found in all the main centres and at most beaches. Keys can be collected at the Jersey Visitor Centre in St Helier, Shopmobility in Sand Street car park or the Town Hall. A refundable £5 deposit is required. See also Beachability (www.beachability.org) who may be able to provide a special wheelchair for beach access. Apart from the Sand Street car park a shopmobility scheme operates at Durrell Wildlife Conservation Trust and Jersey War Tunnels (see www.shopmobility.org.je). Prior booking is advisable.

Emergencies

Dial 999 for police, fire, ambulance or coastal rescue services. The General Hospital at The Parade, St Helier (tel: 01534-442 000) has a 24-hour

Myriad sights to see on the island.

The pound is the official unit of currency in Jersey.

emergency unit. The UK has a reciprocal arrangement entitling UK visitors to free health care in Jersey. The agreement does not cover certain types of follow-on treatment or travel costs, however.

Money

The pound sterling is the currency of the island. Jersey has its own currency, in the same denominations as UK notes and coins, apart from the fact it still has £1 notes. Jersey money can be used on any of the other Channel Islands but is sometimes refused by shops in the UK. Notes can be changed at the airport bank or any bank in the UK. Some shops also accept euros. All major debit and credit cards are widely accepted. ATMs are readily available in St Helier, St Saviour, St Peter, Red Houses, the airport and harbour.

Opening times

Bank opening times are generally 9.30am–4.30pm Mon–Fri, with some branches open 9.30am–3pm

Sat. Most of the museums and tourist attractions are open Apr–Oct, some Mar–Nov, daily 9am or 10am–5pm. The main post office, on Broad Street, St Helier, is open Mon–Fri 8.30am–5pm (opens 9am on Tue), Sat 8.30am–1pm. Normal shopping hours are Monday to Saturday 9am–5.30pm, though a number of shops, particularly in St Helier, are also open in the evenings and Liberty Wharf in St Helier is open seven days a week. Markets and some shops are closed on Thursday afternoons.

Telephones

The code of Jersey is 01534 from the British Isles, +44 1534 from any other country. STD codes for the UK from Jersey are the same as those used in the UK. But if you are using a mobile phone beware that Jersey does not work on the UK system. The networks require a roaming facility, and there are charges for making and receiving texts and calls. Some "Pay as You Go" phones do not operate in Jersey, so check with your provider before you go. The three Jersey

Telephone boxes are painted bright yellow and easily identifiable.

Let's have another round of the local smooth bitter.

networks are JT Global – which has the best coverage – Airtel-Vodafone and Sure. The network extends to the other Channel Islands. Visitors with mobiles will either be linked automatically to a network or can select the network manually.

Tourist information

Visit Jersey (Liberation Place, St Helier; www.jersey.com) has a wealth of information on the island and can also arrange accommodation.

Entertainment

The Jersey Opera House, Gloucester Street, St Helier (www.jerseyopera house.co.uk) stages drama, dance, ballet, concerts, musicals, very occasional opera and children's shows. A registered charity and non-profit organisation, the Jersey Arts Centre (Phillips Street, St Helier; www.arts centre.je) offers a wide range of contemporary and classic performing and visual arts.

Nightlife is mainly confined to St Helier and consists of pubs and discos primarily aimed at young residents.

The *Jersey Post* is the best place to find out about performances by live bands, jazz concerts, DJs, etc. Focal areas are The Weighbridge and Liberty Wharf. The Drift Bar in the Royal Yacht Hotel has a cool ambience, and live music and DJs; Mimosa in Liberty Wharf has a Champagne and cocktail bar and terrace overlooking the marina.

Travel documents and customs allowances

No passport is required for visitors travelling from the British Isles and the Republic of Ireland, but airlines require passengers to have photographic ID. A passport is required if you take a day trip to France. Jersey is not part of the EU, so you can still buy duty-free goods when travelling to and from the island. Maximum allowances are: 200 cigarettes or 250grams of other tobacco products; 1 litre of spirits or 4 litres of sparkling or fortified wines and 4 litres of still wines; 16 litres of beer or cider; £390 worth of perfumes, gifts, souvenirs, electrical products and similar items.

Accommodation

From quirky B&Bs and yurts to to country manors and luxury spa hotels, Jersey caters for all tastes.

To rejuvenate Jersey's image several of the top hotels have undergone multi-million-pound revamps, and a quarter of the hotel guest rooms are now within the 4- and 5-star range. This is all good news if your pockets are well-lined; finding cheap accommodation in Jersey is not so easy.

The self-catering scene in Jersey has been looking up in recent years with more seaside accommodation to rent and, for the adventurous, the opportunity to stay in historic monuments and follies which have been restored by Jersey Heritage (www.jerseyheritage.org/stay/heritage-lets). These range from "stone hut" accommodation in 19th-century seafront fortresses or towers to a stylish 1930s boat-shaped folly on the beach and a panoramic German Occupation observation tower.

You'll be spoilt for choice by the many fine dining opportunities on offer.

To find the best deals book online, either through Visit Jersey or specialist operators (see page 126), or choose your hotel and book direct through them. It's worth comparing costs – sometimes a package through the hotel can work out to be the cheapest option. Typical special offers are three nights for the price of two or free car hire for stays of at least three nights. Off-season room rates can fall dramatically, and there are some great deals at some of the hotels that remain open in winter.

For rooms in July and August book well ahead. Supplements are nearly always charged for sea-view rooms. Check the cost – it's often worth a little extra per night for the fabulous view you could wake up to.

Where to Stay

St Helier isn't the most attractive centre on Jersey, and budget accommodation is limited; but it does have the best sightseeing and shopping, and buses from here will take you all over the island.

Many holidaymakers prefer to stay in smaller centres such as the picturesque ports of St Aubin or Gorey, or on the beautiful beach of St Brelade's. All three have an excellent choice of restaurants and good bus links.

Hotels price guide

The price bands below are a guideline for the cost of a standard en suite double room and breakfast, for two people in high season (July–Aug).
£ = under £110
££ = £110–220
£££ = over £220

Luxurious bedroom at The Club Hotel & Spa.

Hotels

St Helier
Club Hotel and Spa
Green Street; www.theclubjersey.com.
Luxury boutique hotel, with 38 rooms
and eight suites. Chic decor, a swish spa
and outdoor swimming pool, and the
highest rated restaurant on the island,
the Michelin-starred Bohemia. £££
Grand Jersey Hotel & Spa
The Esplanade; https://www.hand
pickedhotels.co.uk/grandjersey.
Swish and glamorous 5-star hotel
where you can sip vintage bubbles in
the Champagne Lounge, dine in the
seductive Tassili restaurant and wind
down or work out in the stylish Elemis
spa and pool. £££
Hotel de Normandie
Havre des pas; www.channelhotels.
com/hotel-de-normandie/gallery.
Good value 3-star set near the
waterfront, with restaurant and indoor
pool. ££
Monterey Hotel
St Saviour's Road; www.morvanhotels.
com/our-hotels/monterey-hotel.
Just a 10-minute walk from the centre of
town, the Monterey offers comfortable
modern accommodation and excellent
leisure facilities. Main features include
indoor and outdoor pools, spa pool,
steam room and mini-gym. ££
Royal Yacht
Weighbridge; www.theroyalyacht.com.
One of Jersey's oldest hotels; built
in the 1930s, now a stylish modern
hotel. Café Zephyr is a favourite of
fashionistas, Sirocco offers fine dining,
the P.O.S.H. Bar is the place for
bubbles, the Drift for live music and
cool ambience. Luxury spa, gym and
indoor pool. ££

St Aubin's Bay and St Aubin
Harbour View
St Aubin's Harbour;
www.harbourview.je.
Charming, relaxed self-catering
guesthouse across the road from the
harbour. Snacks are served on the
garden terrace, and there are plenty of
options for dining out nearby. ££
Millbrook House
Rue de Trachy, Millbrook; tel: 01534-
733 036; www.jersey.co.uk/hotels/
millbrookhouse.
This is a peaceful retreat, surrounded
by 10 acres (4 hectares) of park and
gardens, halfway between St Helier
and St Aubin. Traditional decor,

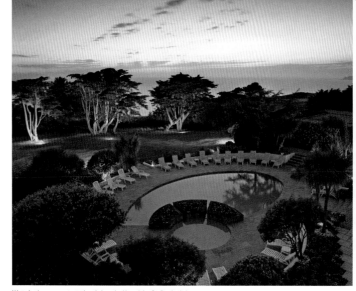

Watch the sunset at the Atlantic Hotel in St Brelade's.

discreet service and very reasonable prices for HB. £

The Panorama
La Rue du Crocquet, St Aubin; www.panoramajersey.com.
Award-winning B&B with fine bay views from picture windows, luxury beds and excellent breakfasts. Non-smoking and adults-only. Plenty of restaurants close by. ££

St Brelade's
Atlantic Hotel
Le Mont de la Pulente, St Brelade; www.theatlantichotel.com.
One of Jersey's most alluring hotels, with magnificent views over St Ouen's Bay and adjoining La Moye championship golf course. Gourmet cuisine is served in a lovely, light sea-view restaurant. Indoor and outdoor pools, health and leisure centre, all-weather tennis court. £££

Les Ormes Self Catering
Mont à la Brune, St Brelade's; www.lesormesjersey.co.uk.
Contemporary and well-equipped self-catering resort comprising

Les Ormes leisure village near St Brelade's Bay and Les Ormes de la Mer coastal cottages, overlooking St Ouen's Bay. Accommodation comes with well-equipped kitchens and king-size beds. Les Ormes has a host of activities, including an indoor (and seasonal outdoor) pool, gym, indoor tennis, nine-hole golf course and fun zone; Les Ormes de la Mer has great surf and stunning sunsets (and the use of Les Ormes facilities). Min 1 week. ££

L'Horizon Hotel & Spa
St Brelade's Bay; www.handpicked hotels.co.uk/lhorizon.
This luxurious and civilised beach hotel has a cool contemporary decor. Over half the 106 bedrooms have balconies overlooking the sea. There's a choice of restaurants, with alfresco dining in summer, plus a health club and spa with heated indoor pool. £££

St Brelade's Bay Hotel
St Brelade's Bay; www.stbrelades bayhotel.com.
Comfortable, relaxing hotel set in immaculate 7-acre (3-hectare) gardens

and overlooking the best family beach on the island. Facilities include a state-of-the-art gym, health club and 20-metre swimming pool. £££

Bouley Bay/Trinity/Rozel
Château La Chaire
Rozel Bay, St Martin; www.chateau-la-chaire.co.uk.
Traditional country house in a secluded spot near the sea at the foot of Rozel Valley. There are 14 luxury, individually-styled rooms, some with en suite spa bath and four-poster beds. The restaurant is noted for fine cuisine, and especially seafood. £££

Durrell Wildlife Camp
Les Augrès Manor, La Profonde Rue, Trinity; www.durrell.org/wildlife-park/luxury-camping.
For something completely different experience the luxury camp at Jersey Zoo. Wake to the sound of lemurs or the sight of gibbons or red squirrels in the trees by your tent. Accommodation is comfy yurts with carpets, proper beds, wood-burning stoves and private bathrooms in separate tents. Cooking equipment is supplied and the zoo has two cafés. Guests have free access to the park and there are additional teepees for children if required. Minimum stay is normally three nights; seasonal. ££–£££

Undercliff Guest House
Bouley Bay, Trinity; www.undercliffjersey.com.
This is an ideal base for walkers, just 20 yards/metres from the spectacular north coast footpath. Bouley's pebble beach, with its clear waters, is down the road. Self-catering, individually styled en suite rooms as well as two- and three-bed apartments and a suite, garden with heated pool and friendly atmosphere. Bus to St Helier. £

Grève de Lecq and Les Landes
Maison des Landes
St Ouen; https://maisondeslandes.co.uk.
Jersey's first hotel designed specifically for guests with disabilities, offering HB, a range of rooms, ramped pool

Fine dining at the Grand Jersey's Tassili restaurant.

Bask in the sunshine on the terrace of L'Horizon Hotel & Spa.

and peaceful grounds. Pickup by accessible minibus from airport or harbour included. £££

Prince of Wales Guesthouse
Grève de Lecq; tel: 01534 482 278; www.booking.com/hotel/gb/the-prince-of-wales.en-gb.html.
Renovated guesthouse and restaurant on this secluded bay on the island's northwest coast. Bus to St Helier. ££

Gorey
Beausite
Grouville Bay, Grouville; https://beausitejersey.com.
Near Grouville beach, the Beausite is a 72-room modern conversion centred on a seventeenth-century granite farm building and is very close to the Royal Jersey Golf Club. Child-friendly, with play area, games room and infants' pool as well as main pool. Self-catering apartments are also available. ££

St Saviour
Longueville Manor
St Saviour; www.longuevillemanor.com.
The highest-rated hotel on the island, this elegant manor house is set in 15 acres (6 hectares) of gardens. The fourteenth-century building has been beautifully restored and is a member of the Relais & Châteaux group. The hotel is renowned for Jersey cuisine and has a heated outdoor pool and tennis court, as well as offering luxury yacht charter. £££

Websites
Visit Jersey (www.jersey.com) has a free online booking service, whether for hotels, B&Bs, self-catering, camping or hostels.

Macole's (www.macoles.com) offers a good choice of apartments and other self-catering accommodation.

Specialist Tour Operators
www.citravelgroup.com
www.jerseytravel.com
www.condorferries.co.uk/holidays-breaks (by ferry only)
www.prestonholidays.co.uk

Index

Credits

Pocket Rough Guide Jersey Weekender
Editor: Siobhan Warwicker
Updater: Rudolf Abraham
Author: Susie Bolton
Picture Editor: Tom Smyth
Cartography: Katie Bennett
Layout: Grzegorz Madejak
Head of DTP and Pre-Press: Rebeka Davies
Head of Publishing: Sarah Clark
Photo credits: Alamy 113T; Alex Cordiner 56/57T, 56TL;
Condor Ferries Ltd 115; Corbis 82/83; Dreamstime 90B; Fish
'n' & Beads 42B; Getty Images 27B, 106/107; Hand Picked;
Hotels 125, 126; iStock 6ML, 12B, 51B, 72B, 74T, 80T;
Leonardo 124; Mockford & Bonetti/Apa Publications 6MC,
6MC, 6ML, 7T, 7M, 7MR, 7BR, 7TR, 7M, 9, 11, 12T, 13, 14, 15T,
15B, 16, 17, 18/19T, 20T, 20B, 21, 22, 23T, 23B, 24B, 24T, 25,
26, 27T, 28B, 29T, 29B, 30T, 30B, 32/33T, 32TL, 32ML, 34, 35,
36, 37T, 37B, 38, 39T, 40T, 40B, 41T, 41B, 43, 44T, 44B, 46,
48B, 48T, 49T, 49B, 50B, 50T, 51T, 52B, 52T, 53T, 53B, 54, 55,
56ML, 58, 59, 60T, 60B, 61T, 62, 63B, 66, 67, 68, 69T, 69B,
70, 71, 73B, 74B, 75T, 75B, 76T, 76B, 77, 78T, 78B, 79B, 80B,
81, 84, 86T, 86B, 87T, 87B, 88T, 88B, 89T, 89B, 90T, 91T, 91B,
92, 93T, 93B, 94T, 94B, 95T, 96T, 96B, 97T, 97B, 100B, 100T,
101, 102T, 103T, 103B, 104, 105T, 105B, 108, 109B, 109T,
110, 111T, 111B, 112T, 112B, 113B, 116, 117T, 117B, 118T,
118B, 119, 120T, 120B, 121; National Trust for Jersey 64B;
Penguin Books 102B; Public domain 18B, 19, 28T, 39B, 82R,
95B, 98T, 98B; Ralph on flickr 79T; Shutterstock 1, 4/5,
8/9, 10, 42/43T, 72T, 73T; The Club Hotel & Spa 114, 123;
The Jersey Club 122; The Pallot Steam, Motor & General
Museum 61B; Visit Jersey 63T, 64T, 65
Cover credits: Mont Orgueil Castle Shutterstock

No part of this book may be reproduced, stored in a
retrieval system or transmitted in any form or means
electronic, mechanical, photocopying, recording or
otherwise, without prior written permission from
Apa Publications.

Contact Us

Every effort has been made to provide accurate information
in this publication, but changes are inevitable. The
publisher cannot be held responsible for any resulting
loss, inconvenience or injury sustained by any traveller as
a result of information or advice contained in the guide.
We would appreciate it if readers would call our attention
to any errors or outdated information, or if you feel we've
left something out. Please send your comments with the
subject line "**Pocket Rough Guide Jersey Weekender
Update**" to mail@uk.roughguides.com.

All Rights Reserved
© 2024 Apa Digital AG
License edition © Apa Publications Ltd UK

First edition 2024

Printed in Czech Republic

Contains Land-Form Panorama Contours & Meridian 2 and
OS Street View data © Crown copyright and database right.

Distribution

UK, Ireland and Europe: Apa Publications (UK) Ltd;
sales@roughguides.com
United States and Canada: Ingram Publisher Services;
ips@ingramcontent.com
Australia and New Zealand: Booktopia;
retailer@booktopia.com.au
Worldwide: Apa Publications (UK) Ltd;
sales@roughguides.com

Special Sales, Content Licensing and CoPublishing

Rough Guides can be purchased in bulk quantities
at discounted prices. We can create special editions,
personalised jackets and corporate imprints
tailored to your needs. sales@roughguides.com;
http://roughguides.com